LESSONS FROM A LIFE COACH

CRAWFORD W. LORITTS JR.

All Scripture quotations are taken from the *New American Standard Bible*®, © Copyright The Lockman Foundation 1960, 1962, 1963, 1968, 1971, 1972, 1973, 1975, 1977, 1995. Used by permission.

Library of Congress Cataloging-in-Publication Data

Loritts, Crawford W.
    Lessons from a life coach: you are created to make a difference / Crawford W. Loritts, Jr.
        p. cm.
    ISBN 0-8024-5526-3
    1. Christian life. 2. Spiritual life—Christianity. I. Title.

BV4501.3 .L67 2001
248.4—dc21

00-054615

1 3 5 7 9 10 8 6 4 2

Printed in the United States of America

*To Burton C. Cathie, my former pastor
and the man who helped start me on this
journey by leading me to the Savior*

CONTENTS

PART 1
The God We Serve

PART 2
Some Fundamentals of the Faith

PART 3
The Inner Life

PART 4
It's All About Relationship

PART 5
The Life That Pleases God

PART 6
Go and Make Disciples

PART 7
God's Faithful Provision

PART 8
A Life Yielded to God

ACKNOWLEDGMENTS

Putting together any book is a team effort, and this one is certainly no exception.

I am so grateful to God for dear friends like Dennis Rainey and Bob Lepine, both with FamilyLife, as well as Wayne Shepherd of Moody Broadcasting, who not only encouraged me to pursue radio but who became partners in translating the vision of this book into reality. Without these people this book would not exist.

I am indebted to John and Peggy Campbell of Ambassador Agency, who have given me a platform to tell what is on my heart.

Linda Waugh, who serves on my team and manages our Website, has been the key player in putting together the transcripts of my broadcasts, which became this book. Linda is one of the most faithful, diligent, positive people I have ever met.

It has been a joy to work on this project with my newfound friend, Tracy Sumner, a wonderfully creative editor who also meets deadlines.

I have loved working with the team at Moody Press. Greg Thornton, Bill Thrasher, Jim Bell, and Cheryl Dunlop not only have become partners in ministry but valued friends and mentors.

My executive assistant, Leonard "Scottie" Scott, has brought a sense of order to the blizzard of activities surrounding my life and ministry. He has also helped me to find the time to make this book a reality.

Then there is the joy and anchor of my life, my wife, Karen. Her love for the Savior and her love and commitment to me have encouraged and inspired me to live what I speak and write about.

FOREWORD

In my lifetime I have had three great coaches. Although they had radically different personalities, they shared three qualities.

First, they continually trained me in the fundamentals. Instructors at heart, they always were developing their players and team in the basics of the game.

Second, they possessed a compelling enthusiasm. I don't ever recall going to sleep at a practice! Motivational masters, these men knew how to bring out the best in an individual and a team. Their love for the game and their players made them easy to follow.

Third, they called the team to a higher goal. The coach of my sixth grade basketball team called us to become "State Champs"—in high school. A college coach challenged us to the National Championship. Each coached every practice and every game with "the goal" in mind.

Although I've never played ball for Crawford Loritts, I can promise you he's a great coach—a *great life coach*.

I've known Crawford since 1980 and followed his life closely. He knows the fundamentals. His enthusiasm is infectious. And he constantly calls those around him to a higher goal. If there was ever a time when individuals needed a life coach, it's today! So if you're going for the gold, you have in your hands the playbook to get there. As I read *Lessons from a Life Coach,* I found myself taking notes. This book motivates me to run the race to win!

But Crawford is more than a *great* life coach—he's one of my close friends.

After living a half century you learn that certain things are difficult to achieve and maintain, like friendships between men, for example. Crawford is one of those rare men in my life who knows me and still loves me. That says a lot about a man.

Crawford's life bears the mark of God's Holy Spirit, and he's a man of the Word. Not only does Crawford do a great job preaching, but his life is his best sermon. He is the real deal! Crawford can speak the truth because he lives the truth. He can call you to do what's right because his daddy taught him to do right! And he can challenge you to trust God in difficult circumstances, because he has endured the storms of life.

So this book must not become just another "door stop" for your library. This is a winning coach's well refined playbook that will equip you to win the game of life.

See you at the finish line!

Dennis Rainey
Executive Director
FamilyLife

INTRODUCTION

On October 4, 1999, the first broadcast of my radio program, *Living a Legacy,* went on the air. The response to this daily, four-minute short feature has been gratifying—and surprising.

I was surprised that people would take the time to respond to a brief program like mine. Almost from the very first broadcast, people began contacting our Website requesting transcripts of the programs. We began receiving phone calls from listeners whose lives were touched by something we said on the air. At various speaking engagements, I began running into people who told me what *Living a Legacy* has meant to them and their walk with the Savior.

The positive feedback I have received compelled me to put in book form some of the transcripts of the program. *Lessons from a Life Coach* is that book. This book is a selection of my broadcasts, edited and categorized for easier reading.

The burden on my heart, reflected in the radio program and now in this book, is that *all* of us, every minute of every day of our lives, are weaving a tapestry out of who we are and what's important to us. Intentionally or unintentionally, we are leaving "footprints in the sand" through how we speak, how we live, how we think. That is what is called our legacy.

Our legacies are not determined at our funerals. Rather, they are being determined right now, as we live day-to-day in our walk with our Lord and Savior. The world around us—our friends, our neighbors, our family members, our coworkers—is watching us and examining every facet of our lives. The question we must ask ourselves is this: Are our lives telling the truth about God?

It is my prayer that as you read this book, you will be overwhelmed by the love of Jesus Christ and that His presence and power will not only enable you to overcome the sin and weaknesses that erode your joy, but that they will be a source of hope and encouragement to those who come in contact with you.

May you know God's richest blessings as you live the legacy!

PART 1

THE
GOD
WE SERVE

"The Lord your God is in your midst, a victorious warrior. He will exult over you with joy, He will be quiet in His love, He will rejoice over you with shouts of joy."
—ZEPHANIAH 3:17

IT'S ALL ABOUT GOD!

When our oldest son, Bryan, was around two years old, he loved pretending he was a preacher. He would put on his bath-robe, gather up his storybooks, and place them on an old milk can we had next to our front door, and preach his heart out. Bryan would turn through the pages in his storybooks as if they were his Bible, but he had only one message: "It's God! It's God! It's God!"

I laugh about that now, but there is great truth in what my son was preaching. It really *is* God, isn't it?

Sometimes we forget that the Christian life is all about God. We have a tendency to reduce our faith to nothing more than a system of beliefs that helps us deal with our stresses, struggles, and problems. But the Christian faith isn't merely a collection of doctrines or moral teachings; it's a relationship with almighty God. It's the all-powerful Creator—the One who made *us*—living within us through His Spirit, empowering us to do His will.

The apostle Paul wanted the Ephesian believers to understand that their relationship with God was not based on their limited understanding of truth. Paul had spent the first three chapters of the letter giving them the theological truths of their faith, but he closed the third chapter with a reminder of who God is. His benediction gave them an overview of God and His awesome power:

> *Now to Him who is able to do far more abundantly beyond all that we ask or think, according to the power that works within us, to Him be the glory in the church and in Christ Jesus to all generations forever and ever. Amen.* (Ephesians 3:20–21)

God made us, so no one knows better than He how to take

care of His creation, how to make it work best for His glory and our benefit.

There's a story, set years ago, of a young man who owned a Model-T Ford. The man was driving outside Detroit when the car broke down. Fortunately for the young man, a limousine pulled up about that time. Out of this limousine came a well-dressed older man offering assistance.

"What's the problem?" he asked.

"My car won't start," the young man answered.

"Well, get in the car and let me see what I can do."

The older man tinkered with the car's engine, and soon he had it running. The young man got out of the car to thank him for his help.

"Thank you, sir," he said. "But how did you know what was wrong with my car?"

"Well," replied the man, "my name is Henry Ford, and I happen to make the car."

No one knows better how something works or how to fix it when something is wrong than the one who made it.

The Christian faith is the belief in and relationship with a God who made us in His image, loves each of us as His own, and takes care of our every need. There is no issue, no need, no problem we can take before our loving heavenly Father that He doesn't gladly meet for us. Can you think of any mere belief system that can do that?

You see, it really *is* all about God!

HERE'S WHAT I WANT YOU TO REMEMBER TODAY:
—◦◦◦—

The God who designed you is the same God who lives within you when you have faith in Jesus Christ.

WHO WAS THIS MAN?

One Saturday morning I answered a knock at our door. Standing before me were two people who were passionately committed to the belief that Jesus is not God. You've heard the arguments: Jesus was a good and wise man, but just a man. Jesus was a prophet, but not deity. I listened politely until they finished, then I asked them if they would listen to me for a few minutes. I then told them God's side of the argument.

"If you honestly believe what you just told me, then you are in a pitiful, hopeless situation," I said. "Furthermore, if you believe what you just told me, what you are doing is an empty exercise in futility."

I went on to explain my remarks by telling them that everything God has designed is based upon the fact that Jesus Christ is God in flesh. If Jesus is not God, I told them, then everything we say, everything we do is futile and a lie.

I finished by saying that I believed that Jesus Christ is the Son of God, that He is God in bodily form.

Jesus Himself declared this reality:

For just as the Father raises the dead and gives them life, even so the Son also gives life to whom He wishes. For not even the Father judges anyone, but He has given all judgment to the Son, so that all will honor the Son even as they honor the Father. He who does not honor the Son does not honor the Father who sent Him. Truly, truly, I say to you, he who hears My word, and believes Him who sent Me, has eternal life, and does not come into judgment, but has passed out of death into life. (John 5:21–24)

The upshot of what Jesus says in this passage is this: "I am one with the Father. We are different in personality and function, but I am God. If you hear Me, you hear from Him."

God came in the flesh in the person of the Lord Jesus Christ to redeem the world from its sins. Jesus took on human form so that He could come to earth as one of us, identify with our sinfulness and weakness while living a sinless life, then die a sacrificial death on the cross to pay the price for our iniquity.

If God did not reveal Himself in the person of Jesus Christ, then what we believe in the Christian faith has no validity or foundation. It would be, in fact, useless. But Jesus is who He said He is, God in flesh, and for that reason we have the promise of eternal life.

What we believe as Christians is not based upon the life of a nice, wonderful man or an outstanding historical figure. It's not based upon the words of a prophet. No, what we believe is based upon the reality that Jesus Himself is God.

We can live a life of hope and obedience to God because the Lord Jesus Christ is who He claimed to be.

HERE'S WHAT I WANT YOU TO REMEMBER TODAY:

The validity of the Christian faith rests upon whether or not Jesus is God. Let's present Him as who He is: God in the flesh.

THE GREATEST LOVE OF ALL

I remember so well how I felt when our first child, Bryan, was born. When I first saw that eight-pound, twenty-one-inch baby boy, tears streamed down my face as my heart was overcome with a love I never thought possible. As hard as it was to believe at that moment, I had the same experience when our other three children were born.

That initial wave of love I had for my kids at their births, although it has changed over time, is still as strong as ever. There's nothing I wouldn't do for them. I would do anything it takes to make sure their needs are met. I daresay I would even die for my children, if it came to that.

But as deep and strong as my love for my children is, it pales in comparison with God's overwhelming, abiding love for us, His children. We can't begin to fathom the kind of love He has for us. It is a love so deep that He held back nothing from us, not even His own Son.

We've all heard John 3:16, the one verse that so well captures the essence of the gospel of Jesus Christ. It's a verse that has been quoted so much that it can lose some of its impact.

For God so loved the world, that He gave His only begotten Son, that whoever believes in Him should not perish, but have everlasting life.

The key word in this beautiful verse is the verb *gave*. God so loved us that He *gave*. He didn't just sit in heaven and cry over our sinful condition, although His heart was torn apart over the path we chose. He *gave*. He gave us the very best that He had.

God the Father, who loved His Son more deeply than even the most loving earthly father can imagine, sent His own Son into this world so He could identify with us, so He could be rejected and despised, so He could hang on a cross in our place. The Bible tells us that Jesus cried out, *"Eloi, Eloi, lama sabachthani?"* or "My God, My God, why have You forsaken Me?" as He bore the sin of the world (Mark 15:34). At that moment, the Father and Son, who had enjoyed perfect fellowship for all of eternity past, were separated for the very first time, by sin. God could not look upon His beloved Son.

I can't imagine giving up my own son to suffer and die for any cause or reason. I couldn't do it. But God did. And He did it because of His immeasurable love for you and me. He wanted to bring us home to Him, and He did just that by sacrificing His own Son.

This is the greatest love of all, the love God poured out on us by giving His Son. It's a love we must respond to, first by turning to Jesus and asking Him to be our Savior and Lord, then by giving Him all that we have so that He may be glorified in us.

HERE'S WHAT I WANT YOU TO REMEMBER TODAY:

We can never repay God for His demonstration of love. But we can show our appreciation by giving Him glory by serving Him.

HE'S BEEN THERE!

My wife, Karen, and I have a daughter who is now in heaven. That fact is a source of great joy to us now, but there was, of course, a time when the pain of the loss of our sweet daughter was almost more than we could bear. We grieved, we cried, we wondered "Why?"

The letters, cards, calls, and visits we received from all our friends and family during that time meant more to us than I can put into words. I still remember gratefully the love and concern our loved ones poured out on us. But we received something extra from those who had personally endured the same kind of grief we were feeling. We had friends approach us who had also lost a child, and they could identify with us more than anyone else could. In a way, there was extra credibility in their words and actions.

There is something special about the comfort and encouragement of those who have "been there" themselves.

Jesus has been there. He can identify completely with our pain. He knew temptation. He understood rejection. He felt the grief over the loss of a loved one. And, on the cross, He endured not just the agony of a horrible death, but a darker-than-dark time of separation from His Father, the One with whom He had had perfect fellowship for all of eternity past. "My God, My God, why have You forsaken Me?" He cried out.

When we are going through something we are sure we can't endure, Jesus understands. When we are tempted to the point where we are sure we're going to fall, Jesus is there. When we grieve over a horrible loss, Jesus comes to our side and comforts us. When we feel so lost that we cry out, as He did, "God, why have You forsaken me?" He knows just how we feel.

That's what I call "divine credibility."

As you read this, perhaps there is some deep pain in your heart. You may be going through something at this moment that you are sure no one understands. Maybe you are enduring the kind of grief that has you walking around in a daze and crying yourself to sleep at night. It may be because of the loss of a loved one. Perhaps it's the heartache of a broken relationship.

"Does anybody care?" you ask yourself. "Can't anyone see how badly I hurt right now? Can anyone understand what I'm going through?"

I want to assure you, He understands! He knows your hurt personally, and He wants to be your source of comfort.

In Matthew 5:4, Jesus said, "Blessed are those who mourn, for they shall be comforted." I believe the primary application of this verse has more to do with mourning our sinful condition, mourning the fact that our sin has hurt the heart of God and separated us from Him. But I believe the Scriptures support a wonderful secondary application to this verse, and it's that in times of pain and sorrow, we can turn to Jesus Christ for understanding, for comfort, and for healing.

And we can do that because He knows intimately the kind of pain we feel. He can do that because He has been there.

HERE'S WHAT I WANT YOU TO REMEMBER TODAY:

Nothing we could endure is beyond Jesus' ability to understand. He wants to come next to us and comfort us in times of trouble.

GOD OF THE COMEBACK

My father was an avid baseball fan, and his favorite team was the New York Yankees. He followed the Bronx Bombers almost religiously, and he loved it when he had a chance to see them in person.

One time when I was about three, Dad took me to a game. Anyone who has taken a toddler to a baseball game knows there's an attention span problem for a kid that age. I was no exception. For most of the game, I was bored and fidgety, so Dad had a hard time watching the game. To make matters worse, the Yankees were getting slaughtered that day.

Around the seventh inning, it appeared that the Yankees were hopelessly behind. So, rather than trying to keep me entertained while mourning the fact that his favorite team was losing, Dad cut his losses and we went home for the day.

He would be sorry he did that.

When we got home, Dad turned on the television to find out that the Yankees had pulled off one of the greatest comebacks in Major League history to win the game in the bottom of the ninth inning.

As the great New York Yankees catcher and manager Yogi Berra is credited with saying, "It ain't over till it's over."

When he found out what had happened, Dad said he would never leave another baseball game—no matter how hopeless the situation looked—until the final out. Even with his team seemingly hopelessly behind, he was going to keep the faith.

Life can bring us situations where things look so hopeless that we want to cut our losses, give up, and "go home early."

But we need to remember that God is the master of the miraculous comeback, that His glory shines its brightest when our situations are the darkest and bleakest.

The gospel of John contains a powerful story that illustrates this point. It's the story of the death of Lazarus, a dear friend of Jesus:

> *He said to them, "Our friend Lazarus has fallen asleep; but I go, so that I may awaken him out of sleep." The disciples then said to Him, "Lord, if he has fallen asleep, he will recover." Now Jesus had spoken of his death, but they thought that He was speaking of literal sleep. So Jesus then said to them plainly, "Lazarus is dead, and I am glad for your sakes that I was not there, so that you may believe; but let us go to him." (John 11:11–15)*

Another way to put that is, "I am glad that you're in a hopeless situation where you have come to the end of yourself. Now I'm going to do something miraculous. I'm going to do something that will make you believe."

When things are at their worst, when we feel that the situation is hopeless, we need to avoid jumping to conclusions. When we are sure nothing good can come out of what we're going through, we need to look to God, who is at His awesome best when things are at their worst.

In other words, we need to let God be God.

HERE'S WHAT I WANT YOU TO REMEMBER TODAY:

Nothing is over until God says it's over. Keep praying, trusting, and anticipating a comeback.

HE WORKS THROUGH EARTHEN VESSELS

We all draw encouragement from the compliments of others. Although we should never serve God or others expecting to receive human recognition, the fact remains that it feels pretty good when someone pats us on the back and says, "Well done!"

After I spoke at a church recently, a man in the congregation approached me and said, "Crawford, I'm so grateful to God for how He is using you. He's using you in a powerful way."

I responded to him with a simple "Thank you." Then he said something that surprised me, something I knew was right on the mark.

"Crawford," he said, "you don't have to thank me. I'm just acknowledging what God is doing through you."

I was grateful for this man's comments, but I was also humbled by the things he said. It reminded me that it's God who works through me and that He is the One who should receive every bit of the glory for anything I do for Him.

There is nothing wrong with acknowledging that someone has done something well or thanking someone for a special blessing he or she passed along to you. Furthermore, it's not wrong to thank someone who pays you such a compliment. But we must never forget that those who do God's work—from the pulpit or podium, from the counseling office, in the mission field, or anywhere else—are only the vessels through which He works.

God is the One who gives us the gifts, abilities, and opportunities to do great works for Him. So the bottom line is, He's the one who deserves all the glory.

In the sixth chapter of John, we read of Jesus reminding

His followers of this point. The people had lost sight of the fact that Moses was, after all, God's servant and just a man. Jesus set them straight on that fact:

> So they said to Him, "What then do You do for a sign, so that we may see, and believe You? What work do you perform? Our fathers ate the manna in the wilderness; as it is written, 'He gave them bread out of heaven to eat.'" Jesus then said to them, "Truly, truly, I say to you, it is not Moses who has given you the bread out of heaven, but it is My Father who gives you the true bread out of heaven."
> (John 6:30–32)

Jesus' point here was not that Moses shouldn't be respected and admired as a great leader of the people, but that the people needed to remember that he was a man who was limited in what he could give the people. What he gave, he was simply passing along from the hand of God, who was and is our provider for all things.

We have a tendency to do with our leaders the same things these people did with Moses. But Jesus made a vital point here about making sure we focus not on the earthen vessels who are limited in what they can provide us, but on our heavenly Father who gives what is eternal out of limitless abundance.

It's good to pass along thanks to those who do God's work, but always remember that God is the One who makes it happen.

HERE'S WHAT I WANT YOU TO REMEMBER TODAY:

God alone is our provider, and He uses people as vessels to pass along His provision. Let us never forget that our heavenly Father is the ultimate provider.

GETTING "USED" TO JESUS?

Around 1993 I traveled with my oldest daughter Heather to the former Soviet Union. It's quite an experience to see the culture and way of life in that area of the world. But what overwhelmed us was the people's hunger for Jesus Christ.

Everywhere we went, people wanted to know more about Christ. The new believers were hungry for the Word of God, for any information they could get about Jesus. The people wanted desperately to know more about the Savior. They asked the most elementary questions and responded with wide-eyed wonderment when we answered.

In short, these people were in awe of the Lord Jesus Christ.

Heather and I returned to the United States refreshed and at the same time very convicted. We both asked ourselves where the awe and reverence for Christ had gone in our own lives and in our culture.

It saddens me to say this, but I believe we get too used to Jesus. We have our Bible studies, church services, and fellowship groups, as well as Christian books, music, and television and radio programs. It's almost as if we overload on the things of Jesus.

We have to be careful that we don't allow ourselves to lose our hunger for Jesus Christ. I believe that can happen when we reduce Him to being simply our friend and Savior, forgetting that He's God of the universe and the Lord of all. Of course Jesus is our Savior, and He said Himself that He calls us His friends (John 15:13–14). But we must remember always that we are to honor Him as Lord of all.

The Bible tells us that some of the people who saw Jesus every day neglected to honor Him: "After the two days He went forth from there into Galilee. For Jesus Himself testified that a prophet has no honor in his own country" (John 4:43–44).

These people had gotten used to Jesus. They watched Him grow up. They had seen Him walking around His dad's carpentry shop and observed Him playing in the road outside of the home of Joseph and Mary. To them, there was nothing spectacular about Him. They may have heard some stories of the miracles He was performing, but they still didn't honor Him for who He was.

Have you gotten too used to Jesus? Have you, even unwittingly, somehow reduced Him to being a pal you hang around with? Have you lost that sense of awe and reverence? If so, then it's time for you to get a new picture of who Jesus is. It's time for you to go to Him and ask Him to renew that heartfelt sense of honor you once had for Him. It's time for you to go to His written Word so you can be reminded of the Jesus we are to love and to honor.

Yes, we should approach Jesus as a friend, as someone with whom we have a personal, loving relationship. But let us never forget that the One we are approaching is the very Son of God, the King of kings and Lord of lords, the Creator of all that is, the One who will judge the world, and the One who gave His all so that we could have eternal life.

HERE'S WHAT I WANT YOU TO REMEMBER TODAY:

Love Jesus and enjoy friendship with Him, but never forget that He is Lord of lords.

GOD MOMENTS

I have a friend who has been diagnosed with Lou Gehrig's disease, a fatal condition for which there is no known cure. I talked to him on the phone recently and asked him how things were going. I was absolutely blown away by how he was handling his condition, by the demonstration of peace and grace God has given him. His faith is stronger now than ever.

I prayed with my friend over the phone, then told him I would pray for God to intervene, either by comforting him as he endured his disease or by performing a miraculous healing.

My friend's condition and how he is dealing with it is what I call a "God moment." This is a time when we know that there is no hope apart from God coming through for us. It's a moment when all doors of human effort have been closed, when there is no earthly hope for our situation.

My friend knows that God can intervene on his behalf and heal him, but he is also at peace with whatever comes his way. His heart is ready to glorify God even if no physical healing is forthcoming. His attitude is that of the apostle Paul, who wrote, "For to me, to live is Christ and to die is gain" (Philippians 1:21).

Have you ever been faced with a God moment? Have you ever been in a situation where all you could do was drop to your knees and pray, "God, if You don't come through, then all is hopeless"?

If you are faced with a moment like that right now, I want you to take heart because God specializes in those moments. He loves giving us hope when all seems hopeless, in displaying Himself in the darkest of situations.

Jesus demonstrated a "God moment" when he healed the blind beggar, as recorded in the ninth chapter of the gospel of John:

As He passed by, He saw a man blind from birth. And His disciples asked Him, "Rabbi, who sinned, this man or his parents, that he would be born blind?" Jesus answered, "It was neither that this man sinned, nor his parents; but it was so that the works of God might be displayed in him." (John 9:1–3)

Jesus healed the blind man, but before He did, He had to set the disciples straight. They wanted to know whose sin caused the man to be blind, but Jesus told them that it wasn't this man's sin or the sins of his family that caused him to be born sightless. That was done, the Lord told them, so that at that very moment in history His glory could be demonstrated.

This story shows us two things about God. First, it demonstrates that His reasons for doing the things He does is perfect. When we are faced with a seemingly hopeless situation, we may ask why. God knows why, and even though He may not do things the way we think they should be done, He knows what outcome in our situation will benefit us and glorify Him the most.

This story also demonstrates that God's timing is perfect. He gives us what we need, when we need it. Whatever we are going through, whatever challenges we face, we can stand back and wait for a "God moment."

HERE'S WHAT I WANT YOU TO REMEMBER TODAY:

We are limited in how we can respond to life's problems, but God is not. We are limited in our understanding, but God is not.

WORSHIPING GOD AND GOD ALONE

My wife, Karen, loves photographs, and she has done an amazing job of putting together a pictorial history of our children's lives. She has pictures displayed all over the house and many, many more in a rather extensive collection of photo albums.

I love looking at the pictures my wife has collected. Sometimes during a quiet evening, I'll sit down on the sofa, open up one of those albums, and enjoy the wonderful memories of our children's lives with us, including our kids who no longer live with us. There are more great times commemorated in those pictures than I can count, and I'm grateful to Karen for that.

Although those pictures are a great way for me to enjoy memories of my kids, I know I can't have any meaningful dialogue with the photos. The pictures are really just recorded images of the real person and a great way to record memories of their development and growth. But I can't communicate in any way with the real person through them.

It's possible—even easy—to do that with God. It's a subtle form of idolatry where we worship representations of God instead of God Himself. The Lord has made it very clear that we are not to worship any man-made image of Him:

You shall not make for yourself an idol, or any likeness of what is in heaven above or on the earth beneath or in the water under the earth. You shall not worship them or serve them; for I, the Lord your God, am a jealous God. (Exodus 20:4–5)

The operative words in this passage are "worship" and "likeness." This means that we are not to ascribe any kind of worship to anything that represents or commemorates God. We are to reserve our worship for the very person of God because He is the only One worthy of it.

I don't think God has a problem with our displaying and enjoying pictures and other artwork that reminds us of Him or His glory. If that were the case, then we'd have to strip the walls of most of our churches and many Christian homes. The problem arises when we give those things honor, forgetting that they are just inanimate images. The question we have to ask ourselves about these things is whether we are ascribing to them value beyond what they are: representations, not the real thing.

We can also make churches, ministries, and even Christian personalities our idols when we give them honor and adoration beyond what they are due as servants of God and not God Himself.

I believe idolatry is a matter of where our hearts are. It's not a matter of what we look at, but how we look at it. It's not a matter of what we have, but how attached we are to it. It's not a matter of whom we admire, but of whether that admiration becomes something that is to be reserved for God Himself.

God will not tolerate the transfer of our worship from Him to that which represents Him. We can avoid that by focusing our praise and adoration on Him alone.

HERE'S WHAT I WANT YOU TO REMEMBER TODAY:

We must worship God alone and never anything that is a reminder of Him.

PART 2

SOME FUNDAMENTALS OF THE FAITH

"For My thoughts are not your thoughts, nor are your ways My ways," declares the Lord.
—ISAIAH 55:8

RELIGION OR RELATIONSHIP?

THE REAL DEAL

A HUNGER FOR RIGHTEOUSNESS

COMING CLEAN

GOD KNOWS!

KNOWING THE FATHER'S VOICE

AUTHENTIC WORSHIP

A MATTER OF THE HEART

IN A CLASS OF HIS OWN

RELIGION OR RELATIONSHIP?

John Wesley was one of the greatest evangelists and Christian leaders of all time. He spoke with great power and won countless people to Christ.

Wesley grew up in a very religious home. His mother would gather him and his siblings around her to pray for them and read Scripture to them. His upbringing had a profound effect on his adult life. He became a missionary, traveling from England to the United States to work to reach American Indians for Christ.

Although he was doing God's work, there was an emptiness in Wesley's heart. He was a religious man. He lived right, and he knew all about the Bible. He had a genuine concern for other people. But something was missing in his life.

Eventually, Wesley came to a staggering realization: He didn't know Jesus personally. He had been doing the work of the Lord for years, yet he lacked in his own life a real relationship with Christ. When he came to the point of knowing what he needed, Wesley turned to Christ for his own personal salvation.

It's all too easy to make assumptions about a relationship with God. We can assume that because we take part in "Christian" activities we know Him personally. But it just isn't so. I believe untold numbers of people make it to church every Sunday morning, attend Bible studies (maybe even lead them), and take part in all sorts of fellowship groups but don't have a real relationship with Christ.

In John chapter 3 we can read of Jesus' encounter with Nicodemus, a very religious and, from outward appearances, moral man. Nicodemus, a well-respected religious leader of the time, approached Jesus and asked Him some very pointed questions about what it means to be "born again."

In verse 3, Jesus answered him: "Truly, truly, I say to you, unless one is born again he cannot see the kingdom of God." Then in verse 5 Jesus told him, "Truly, truly, I say to you, unless one is born of water and the Spirit he cannot enter into the kingdom of God."

The operative expression in this passage is "born." Not "adapt to," not "embrace," not "pattern your life after." "Born" points to an internal work of God through the Holy Spirit that gives us new life. It means that to be saved, we must come to Christ personally, not just conform to the outward expressions of the Christian faith. It means being born into a new life that only a personal relationship with Jesus can give.

To the human mind, it seems so backward that someone could be a genuinely "good person" and still miss out on heaven. But it's true. We can't live a clean enough life to meet God's standards. We can go through life having never lied, cheated, stolen, or hated, and still be lost for eternity. By the same token, no amount of good works will make us worthy of God's kingdom. No amount of missionary work, church attendance, evangelism, or humanitarianism will earn us a spot in heaven.

There is only one thing we can do that will assure us an eternity in God's presence, and that's knowingly, willingly, and intentionally trusting Jesus Christ as our Lord and Savior.

It's all about relationship, not religion!

HERE'S WHAT I WANT YOU TO REMEMBER TODAY:

Our place in the kingdom of God isn't assured by what we do, but by whom we know.

THE REAL DEAL

I recently listened in on a televised panel discussion among some men that got me to thinking about what it means to be a real disciple of Christ. These men bantered back and forth, offering their own insights and ideas concerning fatherhood.

One man spoke up and said, "Just having children doesn't make you a father." Being a father myself, I couldn't have agreed with him more. Without question, there is a lot more to true fatherhood than simply siring children. But what this man said next really grabbed me. He said, "Fatherhood demands involvement, relationship, commitment, and personal sacrifice."

Involvement, relationship, commitment, and personal sacrifice . . . I thought. *Those are the characteristics of someone who is a true disciple of Jesus Christ, characteristics of someone who truly follows Jesus as Lord.*

Just as there is a huge difference between a mere biological father and a real dad, there is a difference between merely placing our faith in Jesus Christ as Savior and aggressively and intentionally following Him as Lord.

What does a *real* disciple look like? What kind of life does that person live? Jesus had a lot to say about true discipleship, and in the fourteenth chapter of Luke, we read of the characteristics every true disciple demonstrates.

First, a follower of Christ must be consumed by love for Him: "If anyone comes to Me, and does not *hate* his own father and mother and wife and children and brothers and sisters, yes, and even his own life, he cannot be My disciple" (Luke 14:26). Did Jesus mean that a disciple must literally hate his or her family? Of course not! This is a figure of speech, a comparative statement that underscores the intensity of love we should have for our Lord. We should love Him so deeply and so thoroughly that our love for anyone else—even our own flesh and blood—should seem like hatred in comparison.

Second, a true disciple is characterized by an identification with Christ's sufferings. In verse 27 He says, "Whoever does not carry his own cross and come after Me cannot be My disciple." Jesus is very clear here that in order to be a disciple, one must be so devoted to Him that he or she is willing to follow Him, suffer with Him, even die for Him.

Third, a disciple must relinquish all ownership and control of the things of this world. In verse 33, He tells us, "So then, none of you can be My disciple who does not give up all his own possessions." This does not necessarily mean a true disciple must get rid of all he owns. It simply means that we are to put our earthly "things" in their place—at His feet and at His disposal.

There's no question in my mind that a revival of true fatherhood would make a huge difference in our world. But just think about how much more of a difference a church full of *true* disciples of the Lord Jesus Christ would make in our homes, in our neighborhoods, in our cities, in our nation.

Are you willing to be a true disciple of Christ?

HERE'S WHAT I WANT YOU TO REMEMBER TODAY:

Real discipleship means giving Jesus not just our best, but all that we are.

A HUNGER FOR RIGHTEOUSNESS

I once read a story about an escaped convict who hid out in the woods for more than fifty days. He needed food in order to survive, but he also needed to keep a low profile. He couldn't very well go to the local grocery store and buy something to eat. So, in order to survive, he "lived off the land." He trapped armadillos and other creatures, ate them raw, and drank stagnant water from ponds and puddles.

It's amazing what an extremely hungry, thirsty person will do to survive, isn't it? In our culture, most of us aren't familiar with that kind of hunger or thirst. For the most part, quality food and clean water are plentiful and readily available, and we've never had to resort to eating wildlife raw or drinking pond water in order to survive.

Sometimes I think it would be a good thing if we Christians learned firsthand about extreme hunger and thirst. I'm not talking about the hunger for physical food and water, but for another kind of nourishment. I'm talking specifically about a hunger and thirst for the true righteousness of God.

In our culture, we Christians can get bloated on things of and about God. We have an abundance of books, magazines, tapes, and television and radio programs that teach us about different aspects of our faith. Most of us have easy access to Bible-teaching churches, where we can go to hear teaching about the faith.

Now, before you throw this book in the trash can thinking I'm being critical of the spiritual materials we consume, hear me out. We are wonderfully blessed to have such an abundance of solid biblical teaching available in all kinds of media. I would encourage all Christians to read quality books, listen to sound teaching on tapes, and attend a church that teaches from the Word.

But here's my point: We must not let these things act as a replacement for a hunger and thirst for the righteousness of God. "Blessed are those who hunger and thirst for righteousness, for they shall be satisfied," Jesus said in Matthew 5:6. What a wonderful promise straight from the mouth of our Lord and Savior! When we hunger for the righteousness of God, we *shall* be satisfied.

So what exactly does it mean to hunger and thirst for righteousness?

It means acknowledging that apart from God we are not righteous, that apart from Him we have nothing to bring to the table spiritually, that we are empty and impoverished. In short, it means acknowledging our need for God Himself.

It's natural for us to become physically hungry and thirsty, but in our natural condition a thirst and hunger for righteousness is foreign to us. But it is exactly what God wants us to seek out. He wants us to search for it daily. He wants us to realize that we need His righteousness every moment we live.

It is a tremendous paradox that it's only when we are filled with God's righteousness that we realize how empty we are, only when we are satisfied that we realize how unsatisfied we are. That's the great thing about God's righteousness: The more of it you have, the hungrier you get for it.

HERE'S WHAT I WANT YOU TO REMEMBER TODAY:

If we cultivate an appetite for God's righteousness, He will satisfy us.

COMING CLEAN

I don't know of many things that are more heartbreaking than finding out that a man or woman of God has fallen into sin.

Several years ago a friend of mine, a man who was involved in full-time ministry, confessed that he had been living a secret life. He had been preaching with great power and liberty, and people responded to his messages by turning to Christ for salvation. Those who knew him looked up to him as an example of a godly man. All the while, though, he was involved in a years-long adulterous affair.

He knew he was wrong. He knew his actions dishonored God and his marriage. In time, the Spirit of God weighed heavily on him.

Finally, he broke the news.

"I'm tired of running," he said to a group of his friends one day. "I know what I have been doing is wrong."

None of us suspected that he could have been involved in something like that. But we listened lovingly and compassionately as he poured out his heart. Our eyes filled with tears as we listened to this broken man pleading for our help.

I'm happy to report that this once-fallen man has been restored and his marriage saved. But that only happened because he was truly sorry for what he had done. He repented for his actions, then submitted himself to a long process of interaction and accountability.

God has blessed this man, but that only happened because he came clean, or confessed his sin to God. There was no rationalization or excuse-making on his part. He called his sin

sin, turned from it, and asked for God's forgiveness.

The apostle John wrote, "This is the message we have heard from Him and announce to you, that God is Light, and in Him there is no darkness at all" (1 John 1:5).

In light of that verse, what should be our response when God convicts us of sin? The answer to that question is found later in the same chapter: "If we confess our sins, He is faithful and righteous to forgive us our sins and to cleanse us from all unrighteousness" (1 John 1:9).

In order to understand the wonderful cleansing that God offers, we need to understand what the word *confess* means in this context. In the Greek, it literally means that we see our sins as God sees them, that we agree with Him about our need to ask for forgiveness and forsake that sin. (I deal with this in more detail in my book *Make It Home Before Dark.*)

We need to see sin for what it truly is. It's not a mistake or a personality clash. It's not a philosophical difference or a character deficiency. It's not an "Oops!" Sin is anything that falls short of God's perfect standard. It's what separates us from a holy God. It's what keeps us from enjoying fellowship with Him. *It's what sent God's only Son to the cross to die in our place.*

We all sin, and we all need to confess our sins. We need to come clean with God and say, "God, I lied. I lusted. I gossiped. I have bitterness in my heart." When we do that, God says He's faithful and just to forgive us, to wipe the slate clean on our behalf.

HERE'S WHAT I WANT YOU TO REMEMBER TODAY:

Forgiveness for sin is readily available to the child of God, but it is experienced only through true confession.

GOD KNOWS!

My mother was fond of telling a story about a very serious question I asked her one Sunday after church when I was little. I had heard something that day that had me more than a little concerned.

"Mom, is God everywhere?" I asked. "Does He know everything? Even what I'm thinking?"

"Yes, He does," Mom responded. "He knows what you're thinking and He knows what you're doing. There is nothing you can do or think that is beyond His knowledge."

Mom recounted that I had a petrified look on my face. Evidently, there were some things going on in my little head or things I was doing that I thought God didn't know about, and I wanted to keep it that way.

Although it wasn't funny to me at the time, I laugh a little when I think about that story now. But as humorous as the story is, it underscores something I'm glad my mother sought to impress on me and my sisters at an early age: Nothing we could do, say, or think was outside God's purview. We may think we are getting away with something, but we aren't, because God knows.

The gospel of John contains an incident that underscores that Jesus, the Son of God, the second member of the Trinity, has complete knowledge of every aspect of our lives:

Now when He was in Jerusalem at the Passover, during the feast, many believed in His name, observing His signs which He was doing. But Jesus, on His part, was not entrusting Himself to them, for He knew all men, and because He did not need anyone to testify concerning man, for He Himself knew what was in man. (John 2:23–25)

Jesus knew the motivations of the people around Him. He knew what was in their hearts and what they were thinking. He knew how they would respond to Him and the things He had to say. And He knows the same things about us.

To know that God knows every little detail of our lives is the ultimate in accountability, isn't it? If we really believe that our heavenly Father knows everything about us, it should change the way we live, the way we think, and the way we speak.

When we take hold of that fact, we will respond to temptation the same way Joseph did when he was tempted to sin: "How then could I do this great evil and sin against God?" (Genesis 39:9).

It's easy sometimes for us to fool ourselves and those around us. But we will never fool God. When we live righteously, God knows. When our thoughts are on Him and on how to please Him, He knows. On the other hand, when we get involved in things we know are wrong, He is there. When we entertain lust or greed or envy in our hearts, God recognizes it.

Although we may resist holding our actions and thoughts up to human accountability, we are still accountable to God. Knowing that, we should keep our thoughts and actions in check. We should consistently ask God to help us evaluate what we do and our motivation for doing it.

HERE'S WHAT I WANT YOU TO REMEMBER TODAY:

Nothing is hidden from God. But He loves us and wants to empower us to live lives that are pleasing to Him.

KNOWING THE FATHER'S VOICE

The spring of 1968 represents a milestone in my life.

It was the end of my freshman year in college, and I knew God wanted something from me. He had placed in my heart a real hunger for the study of His Word, and I was ready to do whatever it took to feed that hunger. Still, I wrestled with the question of what step I should take next. "Lord, what do You want me to do?" I prayed. "Where do You want me to go?"

It wasn't long before I had my answer.

Around that time, someone had told me about a Bible college not far from where I lived. I went about getting information on the college, even though I had no idea if it was where God wanted me to go.

Before long, however, God began orchestrating events to move me in the direction He wanted me to go. It seemed that every time I turned around, I ran into someone who had attended the college or came across some printed information about the school. People who knew I wanted to go to a school where I could study the Word would ask me out of the blue if I'd considered the college.

Finally, events began to unfold to move me toward transferring to the school. I found out that the president of this college was preaching in our hometown, so I went to hear him. After his message, I approached him and said, "I've been interested in checking out the possibility of going to your college."

"Look," he said, "if you will send in the information, fill out the application and all, I will make sure it's expedited."

Expedited! I would have expected him to say he'd send the

information and the application forms, but I was amazed that he said he'd have it expedited. It was as if God was saying, "What do I have to do to make this clearer to you?"

I applied to that college, and the rest is history. I believe that was one of the best decisions I ever made. It was there that I studied and learned the Word of God and also received the kind of training I needed to move into full-time ministry.

God chooses all kinds of ways to speak to His children. Besides using Scripture directly, He uses our own inner desires, circumstances, and the words and encouragement of others. The key for us is to pay attention and discern what He is saying to us through those things.

When God spoke to me throughout that spring, He kept bringing me back to one Scripture verse: "My sheep hear My voice, and I know them, and they follow Me" (John 10:27). In other words, "My sheep—those who have a relationship with Me—hear My voice because they know Me. They know My voice and distinguish it from other voices."

All kinds of voices can get our attention, voices from within us and from the world around us. So how do we know when it's God's voice speaking and not just our own desires or our circumstances? We know His voice because we know Him.

Take the time to get to recognize your Father's voice.

HERE'S WHAT I WANT YOU TO REMEMBER TODAY:

God speaks to us in many ways. We get to know His voice when we get to know Him.

AUTHENTIC WORSHIP

God got my attention one recent Sunday morning. You know the feeling: You're minding your own business when the hand of God taps you on the shoulder and He says, "Excuse me, but could I get you to focus on Me for a bit?"

I was sitting in church during the worship service when it happened. I was "doing" the right things. I was singing the songs and participating in the responsive reading. But my mind and heart were elsewhere. There weren't any major issues on my mind, but I was distracted. My focus was not on honoring my Lord with worship and praise. Suddenly, God got my attention.

After the service, I confessed my sin and asked God to forgive me. I asked Him to give me a renewed sense of focus when it came to worship and praise. I thanked Him for getting my attention and for His promise in 1 John 1:9 that "if we confess our sins, He is faithful and righteous to forgive us our sins and to cleanse us from all unrighteousness."

I doubt if there are many Christians out there who can't identify with my story. At times, we've all found our minds wandering during worship. We may have some pressing life issue before us, or we may just be wondering what we'll have for lunch or whether our favorite football team is ahead.

What distracts us isn't nearly as important as what it distracts us from. When we enter into God's courts to worship Him, we are to leave behind all of life's distractions—the big ones and the little ones—and give Him our undivided attention.

Jesus addressed this issue in His conversation with the Samaritan woman:

But an hour is coming, and now is, when the true worshipers will worship the Father in spirit and truth; for such people the Father seeks to be His worshipers. God is spirit, and those who worship Him must worship in spirit and truth. (John 4:23–24)

In this passage, the word *spirit* is in the lower case, so we know that Jesus is not talking about the Holy Spirit. Instead, He's talking about our hearts' response to truth. He's saying, in effect, "When you worship, I want you to be fully engaged, both emotionally and intellectually. In fact, I want your whole personality to be involved in the worship experience."

Worship that comes from a divided, distracted heart isn't true worship at all. In fact, it's an insult to God. True worship, on the other hand, means yielding ourselves in total adoration for an all-holy, all-loving, all-awesome God. In order to yield to Him in that way, we must prepare ourselves to meet with Him.

When you worship God, you must go with a heart that is ready to meet with Him, engage with Him, and enjoy Him. Your heart must be cleansed of all distractions. Anything that could hinder you from fully focusing on Him—including the biggest of life's issues—needs to be placed on the altar and left there. When you do that, your heart is ready to honor God in your worship.

HERE'S WHAT I WANT YOU TO REMEMBER TODAY:

Worship is a privilege, one we should take very seriously. Let's approach worship with a pure, undistracted heart.

A MATTER OF THE HEART

It's tragic when a once happy, loving marriage cools to the point where the husband and wife go through the motions. The couple may be doing and saying all the right things, but there is no longer any heartfelt passion in their relationship. How sad it is when a union that began with such love—the kind of love that motivates both the man and the woman to do things to demonstrate how deeply they love each other—becomes more of a legal agreement than a love relationship.

I am convinced that if we are not careful, the same thing can happen to our relationship with Christ. Jesus showed us that when He spoke to the Ephesian church in Revelation 2:1–5. It wasn't that the Ephesians—a church that at one time had a warm, wonderful relationship with Christ—were doing anything wrong. Jesus even began this passage by commending them for their wonderful works. Look at His words of commendation:

> *To the angel of the church in Ephesus write: The One who holds the seven stars in His right hand, the One who walks among the seven golden lampstands, says this: "I know your deeds and your toil and perseverance, and that you cannot tolerate evil men, and you put to the test those who call themselves apostles, and they are not, and you found them to be false; and you have perseverance and have endured for My name's sake, and have not grown weary."* (Revelation 2:1–3)

When you read those three verses, you may ask, "What's the problem?" Jesus commended the Ephesians for right behavior and right beliefs. He praised them for holding to proper doctrine and a right standard of teaching. From all appearances, these people were just where they needed to be in their relationship with Christ.

As we read on, we see the problem:

"But I have this against you, that you have left your first love. Therefore remember from where you have fallen, and repent and do the deeds you did at first; or else I am coming to you and will remove your lampstand out of its place—unless you repent." (Revelation 2:4)

It appears that the Ephesians trusted in what they were *doing* right, while at the same time their hearts had grown cold and empty toward Jesus Christ. Jesus' call to repent of cold-heartedness is as timely today as it was all those centuries ago. Christ calls us not just to *do* the right things, but to do them with a heart filled with love and passion for Him.

It can be a struggle at times to keep our passion and fervor for Christ alive. It's easy to get so caught up in "doing" that we forget to keep our relationship with Jesus growing. It's easy to get so caught up in "serving" God that we forget to love Him with our whole hearts and to stoke the fires of passion for Him.

Real discipleship means performing acts of service for our Lord and Savior. It includes behavior that is pleasing to Him and a witness to those around us of His wonderful, sacrificial love. But more than that, real discipleship means spending time with God in fellowship, the kind of fellowship that fans the flames of love we are to have for Him.

HERE'S WHAT I WANT YOU TO REMEMBER TODAY:

Real discipleship means more than doing and believing the right things. It's a matter of where your heart is.

IN A CLASS OF HIS OWN

Do you remember the 1992 United States Olympic basketball team? "Dream Team I" was made up of twelve National Basketball Association all-stars, including Michael Jordan, David Robinson, Karl Malone, Scottie Pippen, Charles Barkley, and Patrick Ewing.

Every game the Dream Team played was a blowout. There wasn't a team in the world that compared with the Americans. With its collection of Hall of Fame talent, the Dream Team truly was in a class all its own.

Our God is in a class all His own. There is nothing or no one who compares with Him. He is infinitely wiser than the most learned human, infinitely bigger than all of creation, and infinitely more powerful than a billion stars. God is far above and beyond all that we can imagine or comprehend.

Although our understanding of God is limited by our humanity, we are never to forget that He is the incomparable Lord of all. God wants us to understand that He is a jealous God who requires our worship. He wants to understand that we are to put nothing before Him, and that we are to put nothing *beside* Him.

God communicated to the children of Israel where their allegiance was to lie: "Then God spoke all these words, saying, 'I am the Lord your God, who brought you out of the land of Egypt, out of the house of slavery. You shall have no other gods before me'" (Exodus 20:1–3).

God spoke these words with credibility, because He had delivered on His promises. He was saying in effect, "I took you, children of Israel, from the land of Egypt. None of their gods could have delivered you, but I did. None of their gods could have saved you, but I did. None of their gods could have protected you, but I did. Therefore, My people, I demand your complete loyalty and allegiance."

Today, God tells us the same thing: "None of your gods could have saved you from sin, but I did. None of them could have delivered you from bondage to your habits and addictions, but I did. None of them had good in mind for you, but I did. Therefore, My people, I demand your complete loyalty and allegiance."

We live in an era when the masses are loyal to their leaders, their belief systems, and their assets. People place their trust in governments, in monetary systems, and in their religions. Sadly, even those who have called on Jesus Christ for salvation can fall into these wrong allegiances.

The bottom line, however, is that none of those things can do anything eternal for us. Only God—this God who gave and gave and gave of Himself so that we could have everlasting fellowship with Him—can offer salvation, wholeness, healing, and eternal direction.

This is a God who not only demands our loyalty, but who deserves it, just because of who He is. God delights in being in a class all His own in our hearts and in our lives. We can give God our allegiance and undivided loyalty because nothing or no one can compare to Him.

HERE'S WHAT I WANT YOU TO REMEMBER TODAY:

We serve an incomparable God, a God who deserves our complete loyalty just because of who He is.

PART 3

THE INNER LIFE

"You gave Your good Spirit to instruct them, Your manna You did not withhold from their mouth, And You gave them water for their thirst."
—NEHEMIAH 9:20

WHERE IS YOUR FOCUS?
DO SOMETHING ABOUT WHAT YOU SEE
PERSISTENT, FAITHFUL PRAYER
KEEPING YOUR HEART STRONG
THE SOURCE OF COURAGE
A MEASURE OF CHARACTER
ENDURING THE PRUNING
BECAUSE HE'S GOD!

WHERE IS YOUR FOCUS?

A number of years ago Karen and I visited my parents on Christmas Day. Our journey to their house was, to say the least, quite an adventure.

On our way to Mom and Dad's home, it began snowing very heavily. In fact, before long we were driving in blizzard conditions. If you've ever driven in extremely heavy snow, you know how nerve-wracking—even frightening—it can be. On this day, I could hardly see in front of me. I slowed the car down to a crawl out of fear that I'd lose sight of the road and crash.

The only thing that kept me from driving off the road that day was that I followed a truck that had its taillights on. It was slow going, but I knew that as long as I focused on the truck's taillights, we'd be relatively safe. Eventually, we arrived at my parents' house, a little worn out from such a stressful trip but safe.

It's important for us to be focused on the right things as we take this journey called life, isn't it? Without that focus, we are in danger of going dangerously off course during the stormy times.

Let me ask you, who and what are you focused on? When you go through one of life's "storms"—a trial or a dark time—do you respond in bewilderment and confusion? Do you find yourself wondering where to turn for comfort, for help? If you answered yes to those questions, then you are likely focused on the wrong things.

What should your focus be on? For the greatest example of godly focus ever, look to the Lord Jesus Christ. Fully God yet fully man, Jesus had to make sure He kept His focus on His heavenly Father. Without that focus, His earthly ministry would have been short-circuited, and we'd all still be lost.

In John 12, Jesus faced the darkest storm in human existence. Before Him was the agony, the humiliation, the isolation of the cross. He knew what lay ahead. He knew that for the first time in all of eternity, He would be separated from God the Father when He took on your sins and mine.

In His humanity, in the torment of this all-important moment in history, Jesus cried out to God:

> "Now My soul has become troubled; and what shall I say, 'Father, save Me from this hour'? But for this purpose I came to this hour. Father, glorify Your name." Then a voice came out of heaven: "I have both glorified it, and will glorify it again." (John 12:27–28)

Jesus is saying, "I don't want to do this, but it's necessary for Me to go through it. No matter how I feel about this, Father, glorify Your name."

That's focus!

In all we do, we must focus on the glory of God. If we take our eyes off that purpose and look instead at the pain, the hassles, the anxieties, and the pressures we are enduring, we will cave in at the moment of truth.

Our souls are anchored when we focus on the glory of God. No matter what storms we are going through, we must stay focused on His glory.

HERE'S WHAT I WANT YOU TO REMEMBER TODAY:

When we go through life's storms, it's important to keep our focus on God, who will deliver us at just the right time.

DO SOMETHING ABOUT WHAT YOU SEE

My mother was quite the housekeeper. She wanted things tidy and in order, and she worked hard to keep them that way. Mom didn't have a bit of a problem making sure my sisters and I did our share to keep things clean, either.

"Boy, why don't you do something about what you see?" Mom would say to me when the house was messy and I wasn't pitching in with the housekeeping.

The apostle James has plenty to say about "doing something about what we see" when it comes to the Word of God:

> But prove yourselves doers of the word, and not merely hearers who delude themselves. For if anyone is a hearer of the word and not a doer, he is like a man who looks at his natural face in a mirror; for once he has looked at himself and gone away, he has immediately forgotten what kind of person he was. But one who looks intently at the perfect law, the law of liberty, and abides by it, not having become a forgetful hearer but an effectual doer, this man will be blessed in what he does. (James 1:22–25)

We can sit in our pews on Sunday morning and hear the Word of God preached, go to our Bible studies, and even read the Word for ourselves; but if we don't apply what we hear or read, then we are wasting our time.

There is incredible life-changing power in the Word of God. James likens the Scriptures to a mirror we can look into to get an accurate picture of what we are really like. We can take a look at that picture, find out what needs to be changed, and, through the power of the Holy Spirit, make those changes. When we do that, James tell us, we will be blessed in all we do.

On the other hand, James points out, we can be like a man who wakes up in the morning and looks at himself in the mirror and sees he needs to comb his hair, shave his whiskers, and brush his teeth, yet shrugs his shoulders and does nothing to make himself presentable to the outside world.

James tells us that someone who approaches the Word of God that way is "deluded," meaning self-deceived. That person can't expect to receive any blessings from God.

Before you go to church, Bible study, or fellowship group, before you crack open the Bible to read for yourself, ask God to illuminate the words to you. Ask Him to show you a picture of yourself as you really are. Ask Him to show you through His Word what you need to change.

God may show you that you have a bad attitude or that you aren't being the kind of spouse and parent He has called you to be. Maybe He'll let you know that you aren't witnessing to the world around you like you should. Maybe He will tell you to pray more and with more passion.

When God shows you what needs to be changed, do something about what you see. Ask Him to empower you through His Spirit to be the kind of person He wants you to be.

HERE'S WHAT I WANT YOU TO REMEMBER TODAY:

God's Word is powerful, but it won't do you a bit of good until you purpose in your heart to apply it to your own life.

PERSISTENT, FAITHFUL PRAYER

In 1988 I had a briefcase stolen while I was at the Los Angeles airport. My wallet, credit cards, money, and all my identification were in that briefcase. But that wasn't the worst of my loss that day.

My briefcase contained some items of great value to me, items that were irreplaceable. It held the Bible given to me by the pastor who led me to Christ when I was fourteen years old. Also in it was a family tree my grandfather had written, which I had just received at the funeral of one of my aunts. Then there was the sterling silver pen and pencil set my dad had given me for my high school graduation.

I was sick over my loss. I knew my chances of ever seeing those valuable items was remote at best. When I returned home, I told my family that my briefcase had been stolen. My son Bryndan, who was seven years old at the time, listened as I talked about the briefcase, and then said, "I'm going to pray that God helps Daddy find his briefcase."

As he said he would, Bryndan prayed every night that my briefcase would be returned. I, on the other hand, had written it off as a painful loss. My homeowner's insurance policy paid for the monetary loss. I bought a new briefcase. I knew I'd never see the old one, or its contents, again.

Then, four months after my briefcase had been stolen, a miracle happened. I received a phone call from a man who told me he had found the case behind his office in Los Angeles. He sent it back to me, and when I opened it I found that the only things missing were the wallet, credit cards, and money. Still in the case, in perfect condition, were the Bible, the pen and pencil set, and the family tree, which now hangs framed in our living room.

I went to my son and said, "Guess what, Bryndan? Daddy got his briefcase back."

"Well, Daddy," he said to me in a calm, sweet voice, "I told you that Jesus would get it back to you."

To this day, whenever I am tempted to give up on praying about something, I think about the faith that seven-year-old boy demonstrated. I also think about what James wrote about persistent, faithful prayer:

> *The effective prayer of a righteous man can accomplish much. Elijah was a man with a nature like ours, and he prayed earnestly that it would not rain, and it did not rain on the earth for three years and six months. Then he prayed again, and the sky poured rain and the earth produced its fruit.* (James 5:16–18)

In some Bible translations, this passage says, "The effective, fervent prayer of a righteous man. . . ." This tells us that simply praying about something once, then dropping it isn't the way to get an answer. It tells us that we must pray with passion, with fire, and with persistence until our heavenly Father answers us.

When we pray, we are to have the same kind of faith my son had when he prayed for the return of my briefcase. God may answer yes and He may answer no when we pray, but we can be assured God will answer us.

HERE'S WHAT I WANT YOU TO REMEMBER TODAY:
—◆◆◆—

We are to approach God boldly with persistent, believing prayer.

KEEPING YOUR HEART STRONG

In 1995 my father died from complications resulting from congestive heart failure. Watching him struggle with this disease the last few years of his life was difficult for all of us who loved Dad. But it was also a warning to me, a warning to take better care of my heart by watching what I eat and exercising regularly.

If we want to live longer and healthier lives, we need to take care of our physical hearts. We need to do the things that keep them strong and in proper working order, and we need to avoid doing the things that weaken them. When we don't do these things we run the risk of sickness and, eventually, a premature death.

Brothers and sisters in Christ, the same is true of our spiritual hearts. If we don't do the things that make our spiritual hearts strong—reading the Word, prayer, fellowship with other believers, and witnessing—then we run the risk of "spiritual heart disease."

When I talk about our hearts, I'm talking about that inner part of us that responds to God and the things of God. It's the part of us that can carry on a relationship with God and can hear Him when He speaks to us. It's the part of us that God speaks to so we can know we are on the right track with Him and following His will for us.

If our spiritual hearts are weak or sickly, we run the risk of spiritual death. I believe that happens to a point even in the lives of those who know Jesus Christ as Savior. And when it happens, it means a withdrawal of God's blessing, direction, joy, and fruitfulness.

God is very concerned about the condition of our spiritual hearts, and He wants our hearts to be pure before Him. In Matthew 5:8, Jesus talked about the importance of a pure heart: "Blessed are the pure in heart, for they shall see God."

Jesus was speaking in this verse of a genuine search to know and "see" the true and living God. He was saying that if our motivation is true, pure, and right, then we will know God and enjoy His blessings. He was telling us that the only way we can fully walk in the power, love, and grace of God is to have hearts that are clean and pure before Him.

People may be impressed with our performance or our abilities, but God is not. He is interested only in the purity of our hearts. He wants to strip away the wrong motivation, the phoniness, the insincerity, and to create within us hearts that are clean, pure, and right before Him.

What kind of shape is your heart in? Is it pure before the Lord? Is your heart sensitive to the things of God? Are you hearing as God speaks to your heart? Look within yourself and answer those questions honestly. If you find that your heart isn't pure, then it is time to make some changes in your life. It is time to look at a new regimen of spiritual exercise and diet!

HERE'S WHAT I WANT YOU TO REMEMBER TODAY:

A pure heart before God is a strong heart before Him. Ask yourself if you are pure of heart.

THE SOURCE OF COURAGE

When I was in the seventh grade, I ran into a problem that too many kids have to deal with: a bully. This young man was a little older and a little bigger than I was, and he intimidated and tormented me mercilessly. He knocked my books out of my hand, pushed me up against my locker, threatened me, and generally made my life miserable.

I never told my mom and dad about the boy, but they suspected something was going on at school. When they found out that I was being bullied, Dad told me what I needed to do. "Son," he said, "I found out about your situation with the bully. The only way you are going to stop him from bullying you is to face up to him. Look him square in the eye and tell him that it stops today."

Looking back on it, what my father told me makes sense. Not at the time, though. To me, it was a classic no-win situation. I could either continue to take the bullying, or I could stand up to this kid and take a beating. Eventually, I took my father's advice. I was afraid, but one day I told the bully that I wasn't going to let him push me around anymore.

Have you ever been afraid to do something God has clearly shown you He wanted you to do? Perhaps He directed you to talk to a coworker about Jesus, but you didn't know how the person would respond. Or maybe He asked you to confront a fellow believer about some situation, but you were afraid that person would react in anger.

I want to say here and now that it's no sin to feel fear. The sin comes in when we allow that fear to keep us from doing what we know God has commissioned us to do.

That was Joshua's situation. He had inherited a mantle of leadership from Moses, who had died before he could complete the assignment God had given him. God came to Joshua and, in a very emotional, moving scene, appointed him to lead His people to the Promised Land:

> *Now it came about after the death of Moses the servant of the Lord, that the Lord spoke to Joshua the son of Nun, Moses' servant, saying, "Moses My servant is dead; now therefore arise, cross this Jordan, you and all this people, to the land which I am giving to them, to the sons of Israel. Every place on which the sole of your foot treads, I have given it to you." (Joshua 1:1–3)*

God was clear in the assignment, but He was also clear in His promises. He told Joshua precisely what He wanted him to do, and He promised him that He had already empowered him to do it.

There is a lesson in this for all of us, and it's this: When God commissions us to do something, He also empowers us. That's His promise, and it's also the source of courage we need to obey, even in the face of our own fears.

HERE'S WHAT I WANT YOU TO REMEMBER TODAY:
—◦◦◦—

We can find courage in knowing God has given us a clear assignment. With an assignment from God comes God's power.

A MEASURE OF CHARACTER

We had a beautiful tree in our backyard. Strong and sturdy, it was functional for shade and a joy to behold. To look at it, you'd think it was the healthiest tree around. I know I did.

One day, however, I found out differently. Deciding to take a break from some yard work, I leaned up against the tree, ready to enjoy the shade, but when I did so this apparently sturdy, healthy tree moved. I examined it and found it was chock-full of termites, those pesky little critters that destroy trees—not to mention houses and other wooden structures—from the inside out. No longer did I see this tree as an asset. Now it was a threat to my home, a threat I quickly removed from the yard.

You could rightly say that those termites caused the tree to compromise its character by slowly tearing down what made the tree strong in the first place. Little by little, they ate at the tree's insides until it could no longer stand up to the elements around it.

That's exactly what happens to us when we allow our character to become eroded or compromised. We may look good outwardly, but inside the erosion of our character will threaten to destroy our very existence.

No doubt you see where I'm going with this. What I want you to understand is that unless your character is strong—free of all "termites," so to speak—you will fall when times of testing come, which they most certainly will.

From the time our kids were four or five years old, my wife and I have made them memorize this statement: "Your character will feed your conduct no matter what your circumstances may be." In other words, you must have within you that which is above you so that you don't become the helpless victim of that which surrounds you.

That made a big impact on me. We become what we associate with. King David knew about these things. Psalm 1 begins an anthology of worship by talking about character. Here's what verse 1 says: "How blessed is the man who does not walk in the counsel of the wicked, nor stand in the path of sinners, nor sit in the seat of scoffers."

I find it interesting that King David begins the Psalms by telling us what a happy, blessed person chooses *not* to do. He doesn't *walk, stand,* or *sit* with those who would compromise his character. David's point is simply this: A person of character steers clear of all destructive influences—wicked people, sinners, and scoffers—that could erode his character. Instead, David goes on to say in verse 2 that for the person of character, "his delight is in the law of the Lord." When he does that, he grows strong in godly character and will be able to withstand the temptations and trials that come his way.

Do you want to have strong, godly character? Character that demonstrates outwardly who you are inwardly in Christ? Focus on what is right and then determine that what is right will penetrate your circumstances.

HERE'S WHAT I WANT YOU TO REMEMBER TODAY:

Good character—godly character—develops when we focus on God and on His law, then demonstrates itself in how we live before a watching world.

ENDURING THE PRUNING

Some very hearty, beautiful shrubs are growing in the front of the Loritts home right now. But they didn't always look that way. In fact, just last year it looked as if those shrubs were at the end of their life span. They had not only stopped growing; they looked downright scraggly. I thought it might be time to dig them up, toss them, and plant something new in their place.

But a friend of mine—someone who knows much more about landscaping than I do—told me just what I needed to do in order to bring those shrubs back to life. It was the opposite of what my own logic told me needed to be done. "The problem with your shrubs is they need to be pruned," he said. "You need to cut them way back and get rid of the dead limbs so they can grow again. They will look ugly for a while, but I guarantee you they will flourish again."

Well, I did as my friend instructed, and he was right. At first, they looked really bad, but when they started growing, they grew with a vengeance. In fact, I have to keep trimming them just to keep them from growing too big.

This principle of pruning applies to our spiritual lives too. From time to time, we have to allow God to prune away the dead, unproductive stuff from our lives so that we can begin to grow anew.

I've learned in my walk with God that sometimes when I'm going through hard times, tests, and trials, it is because God wants to use these painful experiences as a gardener would a pair of pruning shears. It's His way of cutting the unnecessary stuff out of my life so that I can grow and be more fruitful.

I'm not making some novel observation here. Jesus said Himself: "I am the true vine, and My Father is the vinedresser. Every branch in Me that does not bear fruit, He takes away; and every branch that bears fruit, He prunes it so that it may bear more fruit" (John 15:1–2).

When Jesus refers to the Father as the vinedresser, He is pointing out that it is God's job to examine His vines and see what needs to be done to make them more productive. That may include the sometimes painful process of pruning. If something in our lives isn't bearing fruit or is keeping us from bearing more fruit, He shears it off.

This is a great comfort to me, because I know there is nothing I will have to endure that God hasn't allowed. And my heavenly Father knows what I need. He knows what parts of my character and personality need to be pruned so that I can bear the fruit *He* wants me to bear.

I didn't want to prune back my shrubs because I didn't want them to look worse than they already did. But my friend pointed out that they weren't going to bear "fruit"—in this case, beauty in my yard—unless I first made them look worse than they originally looked. But it was for their own good, because it made them better than they were before.

It's like that for God's children when God takes the pruning shears to us.

HERE'S WHAT I WANT YOU TO REMEMBER TODAY:

Going through a pruning experience can be very uncomfortable. But it's another way God demonstrates His love.

BECAUSE HE'S GOD!

I had a tendency growing up to ask my parents a lot of questions. I had a very inquisitive mind, and I always wanted to know how things worked, why we were doing what we were doing, and where we were going.

Most of the time, Mom and Dad didn't seem to mind answering my questions. The exception, however, was when I asked why when they told me to do something. In that case, they'd simply answer, "Because I said so."

There was a tremendous amount of wisdom on my parents' part in telling me that it was because Mom and Dad said so. They understood that children need to learn that there are times when we have to do things simply because those in authority have told us to do them. It was their way of teaching me to respect authority.

Sometimes it's that way with our ultimate authority: God. When He tells us we are to do something and we ask why, sometimes He tells us why, but sometimes the answer comes back, "Because I'm God and I know best. Because I said so."

As Christians, we need to lay hold of the truth that we will have some questions that won't be answered this side of heaven, that sometimes we need to simply obey and lay our faith in the ultimate wisdom of our heavenly Father.

I don't believe it is any sin to ask a respectful why when God gives us a directive through the written Word or through a personal calling. But when we don't receive an answer that satisfies us, we should not be paralyzed from obedience. In that case, we need to cling to our faith in God, obey, and realize that

He has our best interest and His own glory in mind.

Although the Bible is the completely reliable written Word of God, we know that it doesn't reveal to us everything we may want to know. It does, however, tell us all we need to know. John reminded us of this as he closed out his gospel: "And there are also many other things which Jesus did, which if they were written in detail, I suppose that even the world itself would not contain the books that would be written" (John 21:25).

This verse strongly suggests to me that although John—or the rest of the gospel writers—didn't tell us everything Jesus said or did, they did record everything we needed to know to live lives of obedience for Him. What a comfort it is to know that God has revealed to us all we need to know to live a victorious, godly life.

God is not going to answer all of our questions, at least not this side of heaven. But even when He doesn't tell us why, we need to move out in faith and obedience, knowing that His purposes will be served when we do as He tells us.

Go ahead! When you have a question for God, ask it! But remember that sometimes the answer will be nothing more than "Because I'm God, and I said so."

HERE'S WHAT I WANT YOU TO REMEMBER TODAY:

We don't need to know "why" before we move in obedience to God's directives.

PART 4

IT'S ALL ABOUT RELATIONSHIP

Now as to the love of the brethren, you have no need for anyone to write to you, for you yourselves are taught by God to love one another.
—1 THESSALONIANS 4:9

APPEARANCES CAN BE DECEIVING

CONTROLLING YOUR ANGER

YOU'VE BEEN FORGIVEN, SO FORGIVE

WORDS DO MATTER

REJECTED BY YOUR BROTHERS?

CHOOSING FRIENDS AS JESUS DOES

THE GIFT OF MERCY

BACK TO THE BASICS

APPEARANCES CAN BE DECEIVING

I learned a lesson from Calvin I'll never forget.

Calvin was one of my classmates when I was in fourth grade. I met him the first week of class when the teacher led the class single file to the school auditorium for an assembly. Calvin was in line in front of me, and I could see immediately that he walked funny. He walked on the balls of his feet—almost up on his toes, actually—and that caused him to bounce on every step. None of us knew Calvin, so we assumed he was trying to make us laugh by being silly.

Well, we laughed, but it turns out Calvin wasn't trying to be funny at all. Our teacher stopped the line, walked up to Calvin, and said, "Calvin, you're just being silly. Stop walking like that."

Calvin's answer put us all to shame. He said to the teacher, "I'm not trying to be silly. When I was real small, I had polio. This is the way I walk. I can't help it."

I can still remember the teacher lowering her head in shame and walking away with tears in her eyes. She had jumped to a wrong conclusion and said something hurtful to an innocent child.

It's easy to jump to conclusions, isn't it? Christians are especially good at it. We have a tendency to take what we consider our understanding and insights too seriously and to make judgments based on what we think we see in others.

Jesus warned us against jumping to wrong conclusions when He said, "Do not judge according to appearance, but judge with righteous judgment" (John 7:24). In other words, don't jump to conclusions based on what you see, but get all the facts and judge a situation by godly standards.

Jesus was lashing out at the religious leaders of His time who had a dastardly tendency to judge according to outward appearances. They knew all the laws of regulations and customs, and they believed that qualified them to criticize people and judge their spirituality based on how they adhered to the rules.

I don't want to excuse what these religious leaders did, but it's easy for any of us to fall into the same trap. I know I have at times. God gives us a little knowledge or insight, and we think that entitles us to sit in judgment of every person and circumstance we encounter.

When we judge this way, we can do great damage to the body of Christ. I personally can't begin to describe the kind of pain, anguish, and brokenness I've witnessed because of wrong judgments on the part of believers.

Now, there are times when we are right to rebuke, reprove, and correct fellow believers. But when we do that, we'd best be sure of all the facts. We must be certain that we aren't evaluating a situation falsely, based solely on appearances.

Jesus says to us what He said to the religious leaders of His day: Get the facts, ask questions, seek to understand, and go to God's Word. Make sure you are right before you pass judgment, and when you do judge, make sure it's done according to God's standards.

HERE'S WHAT I WANT YOU TO REMEMBER TODAY:

God gives His people wisdom, and we need to use that wisdom, rather than jumping to wrong conclusions or judgments.

CONTROLLING YOUR ANGER

It was twenty-five years ago, but I still remember the lesson I learned from the near disaster in the Loritts home.

My wife, Karen, and I were arguing, and I had become very angry. I felt that she wasn't understanding what I was trying to tell her. We weren't shouting at each other, but the intensity level of the conversation had taken a decidedly upward turn.

I wanted to get out of our apartment to cool off, so I turned to walk out the door. As I did, I passed by our first child Bryan, a toddler at the time, who was sitting in the middle of the living room floor. I walked out the door and slammed it behind me, and when I did the glass in the door shattered and sprayed around the living room floor.

When I heard the sound of the breaking glass, I felt a wave of panic as I remembered that Bryan was sitting close to the door. I spun around to see that my son was surrounded by shards of glass but that he miraculously was not injured. I can still see him sitting there, jagged pieces of glass sitting mere inches from him.

Crawford, your outburst of anger could have hurt your son very badly, I thought.

I was so grateful that Bryan wasn't hurt by my tantrum. And I was grateful for the lesson this incident taught me. To this day, whenever I am tempted to engage in an outburst of anger, God brings that scene back to my mind.

We need to make sure we have control over our anger. Although some Bible teachers and preachers might assert that anger itself is a sin, it is a God-given emotion that has its place in a godly life, as long as it is kept under control. Anger becomes sin when we lose control of it—when it controls us.

This kind of anger—anger that is based on human emotion and not on godly wisdom—is poison to relationships of all kinds. Marriages, friendships, business partnerships, and parent-child relationships suffer and even die when uncontrolled anger is allowed to enter the picture.

The apostle James had this to say about anger:

This you know, my beloved brethren. But everyone must be quick to hear, slow to speak and slow to anger; for the anger of man does not achieve the righteousness of God. (James 1:19–20)

In other words, you can save yourself a lot of trouble if you keep your ears open, your mouth closed, and your temper under control.

We will keep our anger under control when we learn to lend an ear to a situation, then respond appropriately. When we keep quiet and patiently listen to the facts, we keep ourselves from flying off the handle, or reacting in unwarranted and ungodly anger. In short, we must make sure we respond to the facts and avoid reacting emotionally to what we see.

Before you allow yourself to get angry, take a deep breath, count the cost of the anger, submit your anger to the ruling of the Holy Spirit, then respond as He would have you respond. When you do these things, you'll find yourself wasting a lot less valuable time and emotion on useless anger.

HERE'S WHAT I WANT YOU TO REMEMBER TODAY:

We need to allow our anger, like the rest of our emotions, to come under the control of the Holy Spirit who dwells within us.

YOU'VE BEEN FORGIVEN, SO FORGIVE

Dr. E. V. Hill, one of my dear friends and mentors in the ministry, has a great story that demonstrates what grace and forgiveness really look like.

When Dr. Hill was a young pastor, he and his wife had squirreled away what at the time was a pretty good sum of money. One day, someone approached them with an investment opportunity that promised a big return. Dr. Hill wanted to make the investment, but his wife didn't want to risk their savings.

"Honey, this is a sure thing," he told her. Eventually, he made the investment. But the investment was far from a sure thing. In fact, Dr. Hill lost a great deal, if not most, of the money he had invested. When he found out, his heart sank. It was time to face his wife with the news.

Now, any reasonable person would have to acknowledge that my friend had erred in ignoring his wife's warning against the investment. Most of us would even expect her to give him the "I told you so!" business. I know my friend expected that!

He braced for the worst as he walked into their home. He sat his wife down and told her he had lost their savings. When he finished, he sat back waiting for the verbal retribution he was sure was coming. But instead, he heard his young, sweet wife say to him, "It's OK. I forgive you. We've learned a lot from this. Now let's move on."

The young Mrs. Hill knew her husband was truly sorry for what he had done, and she forgave him. She unconditionally let go of the offense and never held it up to him again.

Sadly, it's not always that way. Many times, we're very hard on each other. When someone sins against us, we either refuse to forgive, or we forgive conditionally. We give the offender the cold shoulder, or we continue our relationship with the person but hold the sin over his or her head.

In Ephesians 4:32, the apostle Paul tells us we should forgive, just as God has forgiven us. This is an encapsulated version of what Jesus taught in the Parable of the Unmerciful Servant in Matthew 18:23–35.

In this parable, a servant owed his master a huge sum of money, an amount there was no way he could repay. He approached his master begging forgiveness of the debt, and to the slave's surprise, the master granted him mercy. Immediately, the forgiven slave went out and found a fellow slave who owed him a very small amount of money. The indebted slave begged for mercy, but the unmerciful servant wouldn't forgive, instead having his fellow worker thrown in prison until he could repay what he owed.

In verses 32–33, we see the upshot of this parable:

Then summoning him, his lord said to him, "You wicked slave, I forgave you all that debt because you pleaded with me. Should you not also have had mercy on your fellow slave, in the same way that I had mercy on you?" (Matthew 18:32–33)

We all sin, and we all need unconditional forgiveness. God has granted us that forgiveness through His Son, Jesus Christ. In light of that, we should never withhold forgiveness from those who sin against us.

HERE'S WHAT I WANT YOU TO REMEMBER TODAY:

We all need unconditional mercy at times. Remember that next time you are faced with a situation in which someone you know needs forgiveness.

WORDS DO MATTER

Sticks and stones may break my bones, but words will never hurt me."

We've all heard this little chant, which tells us in essence not to give credence to the thoughtless, even cruel, words directed our way. There is one problem with this saying, though: It's a lie!

True, words won't do us physical damage, but they can hurt us in ways more lasting and deeper than any broken bone. Words can damage our emotions and skew our self-image. They can cut us like a knife, leaving not just scars but open wounds that won't heal, even with the passing of years.

Can you remember a time when someone said something that hurt you badly? I know I've had people say such cruel and hurtful things to me that I wished they'd punched me instead.

While we can't "unsay" the things that have been said to us, we can allow the healing touch of God's Spirit to soothe the hurts and help us to see ourselves as we should.

We can also learn from our experiences and from the Word how important it is to keep control of our own tongues.

James wrote about the power of words:

For every species of beasts and birds, of reptiles and creatures of the sea, is tamed and has been tamed by the human race. But no one can tame the tongue; it is a restless evil and full of deadly poison. With it we bless our Lord and Father, and with it we curse men, who have been made in the likeness of God; from the same mouth come both blessing and cursing. My brethren, these things ought not to be this way. Does a fountain send out from the same opening both fresh and bitter water? Can a fig tree, my brethren, produce olives, or a vine produce figs? Nor can salt water produce fresh. (James 3:7–12)

We really do need to be careful what we say to people and how we say it. Although we need to speak the truth—even though the truth itself can sometimes be painful to the one who hears it—and we need to speak it directly, we need to speak it in a way that is free of condemnation, self-righteousness, and anger.

I can write with some credibility on this issue because I have a bent toward telling people exactly what I think. I have to confess that there is something inside of me that makes me want to give people I think deserve it a piece of my mind, to "say it like it is." I have to be careful, though, because I realize that I am responsible for my words and for the damage, as unintentional as it may be, my words cause others.

I think most of us have a tendency to downplay just how important our words are. But we all need to keep in mind that words have started wars, permanently damaged relationships, and caused untold pain to people God loves. As James points out, it should never be that way.

Let's make sure that our words bless those around us, even when those words might represent hard-to-handle truth. Remember, we are responsible for what we say. Let's always remember to watch our mouths!

HERE'S WHAT I WANT YOU TO REMEMBER TODAY:

We need to make sure we use every word we speak to bless those around us, even when we must speak difficult truth.

REJECTED BY YOUR BROTHERS?

Jesus warned those who stand for Him to be ready for rejection, or worse, from a world that doesn't want to acknowledge Him as Lord and Savior. In fact, He said to count it a blessing when that happened.

But how are we to respond when those who are called by His name reject us because we have chosen to live a godly life?

I talked to a young friend of mine on the phone recently, and he told me some of his Christian friends had cooled toward him. Naturally, this hurt him. He had grown up with these friends, attended church with them, and played sports with them.

"Why do you think they are stepping back from you?" I asked. "Is it possible there is something you've done or said that hurt or offended them?"

He told me his friends were professing Christians, but that their lifestyles didn't honor God, that they were into certain activities that he knew didn't please the Lord. This young man is not perfect by any stretch of the imagination. But he is growing in his relationship with God and seeks to serve Him in how he lives, how he talks, and how he thinks.

I had a hunch what the problem was. "I can't say for sure because I don't know your friends, but I think the problem may be that the way you live makes them uncomfortable because they aren't living right," I said. "When you have a sincere desire to walk with the Lord and represent Him, people who don't want to do that have a tendency to attack the messenger, because they don't want to hear what that person has to say. I think that maybe their hearts are convicted, and you are a reminder that they need to change."

If you've ever been on the other side of that, you understand what I mean. When the Lord is dealing with some area of your life and you are resistant to His promptings for change, it is difficult to be around people who have submitted that particular area to Him. They are irritating reminders that you need to make a change, and you may find yourself avoiding them.

Jesus was rejected by those who didn't want to be reminded of their need for change, including some who were close to Him:

> *For not even His brothers were believing in Him. So Jesus said to them, "My time is not yet here, but your time is always opportune. The world cannot hate you, but it hates Me because I testify of it, that its deeds are evil." (John 7:5–7)*

When our lives honor Christ, those whose lives don't honor Him will find it difficult to be around us. Sadly, that may include some who are in church every Sunday morning. When that happens, first count it as a blessing. Remember that those who lived sinful lives hated Him, and they're going to hate you. Second, remember to pray for those who need to get right with Him. Third, be sure that you aren't responding to others in a proud spirit or critiquing them with extrabiblical codes of conduct. Finally, keep living a life that pleases God. It may be an irritant to those who don't want to repent, but it will also be a reminder of Jesus' power to forgive and restore.

HERE'S WHAT I WANT YOU TO REMEMBER TODAY:

When we live in a way that pleases God, we may make those around us uncomfortable, including those sitting next to us at church.

CHOOSING FRIENDS AS JESUS DOES

Some time ago I attended a national convention of prominent Christian leaders and personalities. I guess in some circles it could have been considered a "who's who" meeting.

One night at this convention, I had an appointment to meet with a friend, so I went to the lobby to wait for him. As I waited, I spotted an acquaintance I hadn't seen in quite a long time, so I walked up to him to say hello. As we chatted, it wasn't long before I noticed that he didn't seem all that interested in our conversation. He kept looking past me, as if he was looking for someone else. Soon it became quite obvious what was going on: This man wasn't interested in talking to me; rather, he was looking to meet and associate with some more "recognized" people, people with bigger names than mine.

At first, I felt a little put off, but then I realized it was a sad and funny reminder of one negative in human nature: We tend to want to associate with those who can "do" something for us, those who impress us with their reputations or positions, those we find attractive or desirable. I've done it myself.

Let me say now that I believe this is a sinful attitude.

First of all, people are made in God's image, and they are all important, no matter who they are or what their position. God does not see the layperson who ministers to only a few people each week as being any less valuable than the leader of a huge television or radio ministry that reaches millions.

Second, I believe it is wrong to place more importance on people in higher positions, because it is God who has put them in those positions, for His will and purposes. It is no more right for us to inflate their value to God than it is for them to do so.

Jesus addressed this, and He did it while sitting in the house of a very prominent Pharisee:

> *And He began speaking a parable to the invited guests when He noticed how they had been picking out the places of honor at the table, saying to them . . . "For everyone who exalts himself will be humbled, and he who humbles himself will be exalted. . . . But when you give a reception, invite the poor, the crippled, the lame, the blind, and you will be blessed, since they do not have the means to repay you; for you will be repaid at the resurrection of the righteous."* (Luke 14:7, 11, 13–14)

Jesus' point in this passage is not "Don't associate with people of means." His point is that we shouldn't associate with prominent people just so we can get something from them, that we shouldn't lose sight of the fact that each person has value in God's sight.

God will bless you with what He has for you, in His time and in His way. In the meantime, don't reach out to people of means or prominent people while overlooking those in a "lower" station in life.

Look to be a blessing to each person you meet, no matter what his or her position may be.

HERE'S WHAT I WANT YOU TO REMEMBER TODAY:

We shouldn't be respecters of position or status. We need to examine our motivation when we make associations with people around us.

THE GIFT OF MERCY

I was guilty and I knew it. There was no contesting the facts of the incident. I knew nothing I could honestly say would change my guilt.

Several years back, I was driving with my wife and children down the interstate during our family vacation, and I had gotten some lead in my feet. In other words, I was speeding, and more than a few miles an hour over the limit.

I looked in the rearview mirror just in time to see the flashing blue lights. It was a state trooper, and he had me dead to rights. I was at his mercy. I gave the officer my license, then began fumbling through the glove compartment to get my insurance card. All the while, I prepared myself for the worst.

"You know you were speeding," the officer said, then glanced in the back seat of the car, where my children were seated.

"Are you going on a vacation?" the police officer asked.

"Yes sir," I answered. "We are."

"I see you have your family with you," he said.

"Yes sir," I answered. I felt terrible because not only was I speeding, but I was doing it with my wife and children in the car. I was sure the officer was going to lower the boom on me. I knew I had it coming.

Then, out of the blue, the officer said, "I'm not going to give you a ticket this time. I'm going to give you a warning. But be careful, slow down, and drive safely. Have a nice day."

As the officer walked back to his patrol car and drove off, one of my children asked, "Dad, did you get a ticket?"

"No," I replied, "I didn't get a ticket. I got mercy."

This story demonstrates to me what mercy really is. When someone shows mercy, he does it by not doing to another person what that person truly deserves.

Those of us who know Jesus Christ as Savior won't be getting something we all have coming to us: God's eternal judgment. We will escape the condemnation we as sinners so richly deserve simply because God the Father has poured out His mercy on us by sending His Son to take the punishment that would have been ours.

In light of the mercy we have received, how can we do any less with those around us? Jesus pointed that out in Matthew 5:7, when he said, "Blessed are the merciful, for they shall receive mercy."

God doesn't pour out His love and mercy on us expecting that we'll just soak it in, enjoy it, and keep it to ourselves. We've been given mercy, and we are to give it to others in kind.

When we think of showing mercy, we usually think of forgiving those who have wronged us or offended us. That's certainly part of it, but there are any number of other ways we can show mercy to those around us.

We can start by telling them about the ultimate act of mercy: when God the Father extended unmerited forgiveness by giving us His Son, the Lord Jesus Christ.

HERE'S WHAT I WANT YOU TO REMEMBER TODAY:

We are blessed most when we show mercy to those around us. The world is full of people who desperately need that mercy.

BACK TO THE BASICS

I love the game of golf. Anyone who has played the game knows that the key to enjoying golf is to have success at it. And the key to that success is mastering a few of the basics of the game.

I've learned that when I play poorly it's almost always a matter of something I'm doing wrong. In that case, I have to revisit the basics of the game, then correct my error. For example, I'll ask myself if I kept my head down during my swing, or if I was lined up on the ball properly. Usually, when I go back to the basics and make the corrections I need to make, I start hitting the ball straight.

Sometimes the Christian faith requires us to get back to the basics. I believe that is what Jesus was calling the church to do when He spoke these words to the Ephesian church in Revelation 2:4–5:

But I have this against you, that you have left your first love. Therefore remember from where you have fallen, and repent and do the deeds you did at first.

I believe Jesus is saying in this passage, "When you feel like things have fallen apart and there's dryness in your heart, slow down a little bit. Remember the basics." In other words, go back beyond your Christian activity, beyond your insights about the Scriptures, and remember who delivered you from your sins and made you a new person. In short, go back to that relationship with Jesus.

Sometimes I think we complicate Christianity. We get so wound up in "doing" and "being" that we forget that the essence of our faith is simply a loving relationship with Jesus Christ.

Do you need to get back to the basics of your faith? Start by thinking about how it was when you first trusted Christ. You probably didn't know much about the Bible or doctrine or theology. You didn't know much about what you should or shouldn't do. You just knew that you loved Jesus.

I'll never forget when I first trusted Christ as a teenager. When I went to bed, I didn't want to fall asleep because I wanted to just talk to Him in the quietness of the night. I didn't know what to say or how to pray. I didn't understand the theology of what had happened to me. I just knew that I loved Him. To this day, I am aware of my need to take myself back to that time, when all I knew to tell Jesus was how much I loved Him.

When you find yourself in a dry time in your faith, get back to the basics. Remember when you first came to Christ. For just a moment, lay aside a focus on doctrine only, Christian service, or what you should be doing and concentrate on how much you love Him. Tell Him how much you love Him, how grateful you are for what He has done for you. You'll be amazed how quickly that time of dryness will become nothing but a memory.

HERE'S WHAT I WANT YOU TO REMEMBER TODAY:

A personal love relationship between ourselves and Jesus Christ is what the Christian faith is all about. Remember always to tell Him how much you love Him.

PART 5

THE LIFE THAT PLEASES GOD

Sow with a view to righteousness,
Reap in accordance with kindness;
Break up your fallow ground,
For it is time to seek the Lord
Until He comes to rain righteousness on you.
—HOSEA 10:12

TRUE TO YOUR WORD

My father was a man of impeccable integrity. I wrote about him in my book *Never Walk Away*. In fact, the subtitle of the book, "Lessons of Integrity from a Father Who Lived It," really is his signature on my life.

To my father, a person's word was the measure of his or her integrity. He used to say, "You can talk all you want, but if you don't measure up to what you said, then you're not really much of a person." Dad believed that people shouldn't make casual statements or promises. He didn't even believe in signing contracts. If you said you were going to do something, your word was your guarantee, and you did it. Period.

My dad never made a promise to his kids that he didn't keep. If he promised to take me to a ball game and then found out he had to work, he didn't just break the promise. Instead, he'd come to me and say, "Son, I found out that I have to work, so let's reschedule." And I never had to worry about whether he'd make good on his word. I'd grown up counting on it.

We live in a day when a person's word isn't worth a lot. It's gotten to the point that we need an army of lawyers to keep track of what was said by all parties in a business agreement. People headed to the altar of marriage are signing prenuptial agreements, which protect one or both parties' assets in the event—an increasingly likely event—of divorce.

I understand as well as anyone the need for contracts and other written agreements in this day and age. But what bothers me about these things is they seem to have replaced our word as a binder for those we deal with, and contracts themselves seem increasingly easy to break.

James made some sobering comments about the importance of keeping our word. Look at what James said:

But above all, my brethren, do not swear, either by heaven or by earth or with any other oath; but your yes is to be yes, and your no, no, so that you may not fall under judgment. (James 5:12)

The last line in that verse—*so that you may not fall under judgment*—should really grab our attention. It tells us that God judges the words that we speak and whether we are true to those words. That should motivate us to carefully measure what we say and our intent for saying it.

Integrity is very important to God. He does not approve of His people using inaccurate statements. He does not want us trying to deceive by any kind of word or action. And when we give our word—when we tell someone we are going to do something—we'd better stick by it and do what we said we would.

Have you made promises that you haven't kept? Have you tried to weasel out of a commitment you made? In our culture, getting out of agreements with others may be as easy as calling a lawyer to examine the contract for loopholes. But in God's eyes, you are not released from verbal commitments or promises, no matter who declares them "null and void."

It's as simple as this: If you say you'll do something, then do it!

HERE'S WHAT I WANT YOU TO REMEMBER TODAY:

Our credibility as Christians should reflect God's credibility, and He demands that we follow through on our commitments and promises.

A "DIVISIVE" LIFESTYLE

Have you ever known someone who came to Christ, only to have those who were close to that person back away? Maybe that happened to you when you made a statement of faith.

Something about living for Jesus can make those around us a little uncomfortable. They may even find our changed lives and focus something of an irritant. Although there will be some who seek out the company of a Christian because they are interested in knowing about Christ, there are usually more who avoid people who serve the Lord. I have seen people whose friends and family ridiculed, mocked, or even rejected them when they came to the Lord. I've even seen spouses leave their marriages when their partner turned to Christ.

Although it is uncomfortable and painful when that happens, we have to remember that Jesus said it comes with the territory:

Do you suppose that I came to grant peace on earth? I tell you, no, but rather division; for from now on five members in one household will be divided, three against two and two against three. They will be divided, father against son and son against father, mother against daughter and daughter against mother, mother-in-law against daughter-in-law and daughter-in-law against mother-in-law. (Luke 12:51–53)

This does not mean that Jesus came to be the author of confusion in this world. He was simply saying that those who come to Him will be different. They will think differently, speak differently, and behave differently, and that difference will be the source of conviction for those who refuse to repent. Sinners may not even fully understand why they feel so uncomfortable—even hostile—when they are around committed Christians. They may not realize that they are seeing in that believer what they lack in their own lives. All they know is that there's something disquieting about that person, something that makes them feel uneasy.

Unfortunately, our Christian culture has done its best to package and market Christianity in a "seeker-friendly" package. We often present a gospel that brings harmony, comfort, and acceptance from others in this life. But that is not the Christianity presented in the Scriptures.

Take the time to read the book of Acts, and you will see accounts of people facing rejection and persecution—even to the point of death in many cases—for their Christian testimonies. The book of Acts is full of accounts of the apostles being arrested, imprisoned, threatened with death, beaten, and stoned for their statements of faith.

Jesus never said standing up for Him would be an easy path to take. We should never make the mistake of believing that, and we should never present a gospel that leaves someone with that impression.

The gospel of Jesus Christ brings peace—peace with Him and with other believers—to those who are open to the Prince of Peace. But it brings division and animosity from those who reject the Savior and refuse to repent.

Don't be surprised when people reject you, or do worse, when you stand for Christ. Remember, Jesus never promised us harmony with those around us who are of this world, nor should we expect it. Count it a blessing to be worthy of the world's animosity because of your walk with Christ.

HERE'S WHAT I WANT YOU TO REMEMBER TODAY:

Peace with God through Christ means animosity from the world. We shouldn't be surprised when we run into opposition because of the life we live.

THE STATE OF THE FAITH

A number of years ago I bought a lemon of a used car. It appeared to be a quality automobile. It looked and sounded great. It was loaded with accessories I couldn't have afforded in a new car. Appearances can be deceiving, however, and during the first year I owned that car it spent more time in the shop than it did on the road.

Sadly, Christians out there in droves are like that car. They look good on the surface, but something is terribly wrong inside. Oh, they say the right things and even do some of the things we associate with the faith. But when it gets right down to it, they aren't living a life that pleases God.

It grieves me to say this, but in too many ways the lives of a lot of Christians aren't any different from the lives of those who don't profess faith in Jesus. That isn't just my opinion, either. The numbers back me up on this one.

A few years ago George Barna, the well-known Christian pollster and researcher, polled thousands of professing Christians concerning their lifestyles. He asked them questions about areas such as marital fidelity, honesty, their use of free time, and what they did with their money and time. Barna concluded that in sixty-six lifestyle categories, the lives of the Christians were not appreciably different from those of unbelievers.

God has set His people apart and called them to be different from the world. We are to live differently and think differently. Our lives are supposed to be built around the truths of God's Word. But it isn't happening, not in the lives of *most* professing Christians anyway.

I hear a lot of talk about spiritual revival in our culture in this day, but I have to wonder if it's really happening. Sure, there are pockets of revival, some of which I have been privileged to witness and take part in myself. But is there really a widespread revival taking place that results in changed lives within the church?

There's no question in my mind that we need God to touch us with revival. We need His Spirit to move on us and transform our hearts and minds and give us a new fire to be the people He has called us to be. We need to repent of conforming ourselves to this world and ask God to conform us to the image of His Son, Jesus Christ.

We need to pray as the prophet Habakkuk prayed when he saw the need for revival: "Lord, I have heard the report about You and I fear. O Lord, revive Your work in the midst of the years, in the midst of the years make it known; in wrath remember mercy" (Habakkuk 3:2).

Habakkuk knew that God was holy and just, and that sooner or later He would judge the people's sin. But he also knew that God was a loving, merciful God who desired to pour out revival on His people. This was true during Habakkuk's time, and it's still true.

God wants to touch the hearts of His people with revival, with a renewed fire for Him. Let us pray for that revival today and every day!

HERE'S WHAT I WANT YOU TO REMEMBER TODAY:

If we are going to make a difference in the world around us, we need revival. Let's pray for the fire of revival to sweep through the church today.

A GODLY APPROACH TO WEALTH

I have a friend who is a very successful businessman. In fact, he's a little more than successful; he's actually quite wealthy. If you were to meet this man, however, you would never guess he is rich. He's very humble. There is no air of big money around him.

I like to say that my friend is the way he is because he has not allowed what he possesses to possess him. There's sort of a detachment between him and his money, and that is because he sees it as a resource the Lord has given him to further God's kingdom through generous financial support of various ministries and missionary organizations.

I had lunch with this dear old friend of mine recently, and he said something that greatly blessed me. He looked me right in the eye and said, "Crawford, God has blessed me with the ability to make money, not for myself, but for His cause. I have to trust Him just like everybody else does."

Talk about godly motivation! Here's a man who is worth more than most of us will make in a lifetime, and he takes the approach that nothing in his bank account is his, but that it belongs to God.

The apostle James points out that no matter what our station in life—whether we are well-to-do or just getting by—our motivation for all we do should be to glorify God:

> But the brother of humble circumstances is to glory in his high position; and the rich man is to glory in his humiliation, because like flowering grass he will pass away. For the sun rises with a scorching

wind and withers the grass; and its flower falls off and the beauty of its appearance is destroyed; so too the rich man in the midst of his pursuits will fade away. (James 1:9–11)

At first glance, it appears that James is putting down material wealth. But when you examine this text more closely, you can see that is not what he's talking about at all. What he's condemning is the attachment to things. He's saying that the rich man has the same basic needs as the poor man and that everything in this life, including monetary wealth, will fade away and mean nothing when we stand before God.

We live in a society that worships at the shrine of the almighty dollar. We pay tremendous respect to those who have great material wealth. In our culture, money paves your way to status, significance, and recognition.

My wealthy friend is getting along in years now, and he's figured out something we all need to lay hold of: Whether we have the wealth of a king or we live hand-to-mouth, our value is the same to almighty God. Wealth will pass away, but our relationship with God must remain a constant in our lives.

The bottom line is, whether we are rich or poor, we have to trust God daily for His provision. And whatever position He puts us in financially, our responsibility is the same: We are to glorify Him with all that we have.

HERE'S WHAT I WANT YOU TO REMEMBER TODAY:

No matter what our station or status in this life may be, we must trust God, rely on God, and glorify God.

THE SOURCE OF SIN

I was doing what Mom had told me not to do when disaster struck.

I was about nine years old, and my parents had gone out and left me and my sisters home. My sisters couldn't follow me everywhere, so there I was, in the living room, doing what Mom had told me not to do: swing my baseball bat in the house.

I was having a ball, doing my best imitation of Willie Mays, when it happened. I got too close to the lamp on the end table, and my bat bumped the lamp. It fell to the floor and shattered.

When my sisters heard the ruckus, they rushed into the living room and saw the aftermath. "What happened?" they asked. It didn't take a crack detective to see what had just occurred. I was standing there with my bat in my hand, and what had once been a lamp lay on the floor in pieces. Still, I tried to cover my tracks.

"I don't know," I said. "The lamp just fell."

When my parents came home, Dad started asking me questions about what had happened. I stuck to my story, but Dad knew better. "Son," he said, "lamps don't just fall. That lamp was nowhere near the edge of the table. So what happened?"

Finally, I broke down and told the truth.

What do you think made me lie? Why did I try to cover my tracks when I knew very well what I had done? Was it the devil? Well, the devil is the father of lies, but he didn't make me lie. I lied to my sisters then my father for the same reason any of us sins: the old sin nature.

James outlined the process of sin in our lives when he wrote:

Let no one say when he is tempted, "I am being tempted by God"; for God cannot be tempted by evil, and He Himself does not tempt anyone. But each one is tempted when he is carried away and enticed by his own lust. Then when lust has conceived, it gives birth to sin; and when sin is accomplished, it brings forth death. (James 1:13–15)

A number of years ago, I heard an old preacher say you have to feel sorry for the devil because he gets blamed for so much of our sinfulness. I don't know if I would go quite that far, but the old preacher's point is a valid one. We really do tend to erroneously blame Satan for our sin.

An old hymn puts it this way: "Prone to wander, Lord I feel it, prone to leave the God I love." In other words, that proneness to sin is part of us, part of our nature.

Satan does tempt us with sin, but we choose whether or not to give into that temptation. That was what happened in the Garden of Eden. The devil didn't force Adam and Eve to sin; he can't do that. They chose the path of sin, and we've been choosing that path ever since.

We need to grasp the fact that sin is our choice. When we understand that, when we take responsibility for our sin, we are one step closer to overcoming that sin.

HERE'S WHAT I WANT YOU TO REMEMBER TODAY:

It's easy to blame others for our sin. We need to lay hold of the fact that it's our choice whether or not to give into temptation.

WHAT'S YOUR MOTIVATION?

I came home from the office one evening, very tired after a very long, busy day. Our youngest daughter Holly picked up on how weary I was, and she started playing the role of comforter. She rubbed my head, hugged me, and kissed me on the cheek. "Dad, you look tired, so just sit down and relax," she said, then went and got me a cup of coffee.

"You know, Dad," she said, as she served up the cup, "you are the best daddy in the world."

I smelled the setup. Actually, I saw it coming when she first greeted me that evening. She wanted something from me, so she was buttering me up.

I have to admit that I'm kind of a soft touch that way. I walk into situations like that with my eyes wide open. When my daughter does that, I know I'm being had, but I give in to what she wants. In a way, it's her sweet and innocent way of pulling the wool over my eyes.

I think we sometimes not-so-sweetly and not-so-innocently try to pull the wool over our Lord's eyes. By that I mean we follow Jesus with the wrong motivation, namely to get what we want from Him. Instead of treating Him as the Lord of our lives, we treat Him as a cosmic banker who comes in to rescue us when we need it.

It's very foolish to do that, when you think about it. After all, the God we're talking about here is One who knows everything, including our motives. In other words, *we can't pull the wool over His eyes.*

I believe that God wants us to be totally dependent on

Him in every area of our lives. But I also believe we need to constantly examine our hearts to make sure that our motivations for seeking His favor are right. We must ask ourselves if we are following Him out of love and commitment, or just because we want something from Him.

In John 6:26, we read of how Jesus addressed the issue of wrong motivation for following Him: "Jesus answered them and said, 'Truly, truly, I say to you, you seek Me, not because you saw signs, but because you ate of the loaves and were filled.'"

In other words, Jesus was telling them, "You are not following Me because you really believe in Me or because of a heart's desire to lay down your life for Me. It's not Me you are coming after, but what I can provide for you."

In the next verse, the Lord addressed proper motivation for following Him: "Do not work for the food which perishes, but for the food which endures to eternal life, which the Son of Man will give to you, for on Him the Father, God, has set His seal."

Jesus' message here is clear. Sure, He can provide for our physical needs and perform miracles. But we are not to follow Him because of those things, but rather because of who He is. Yes, we should pray and ask God to meet our physical needs, but our primary motivation to follow Him must be based on the eternal.

HERE'S WHAT I WANT YOU TO REMEMBER TODAY:

We should follow Jesus not for what He does for us, but for who He is.

FLYING OVER THE RIGHT TARGET

I have a friend who served as a fighter pilot during the Vietnam War. If there's one thing I will always remember him telling me about flying in the war, it's this: "You know you're flying over the right target when you're being shot at."

That statement is memorable to me because it makes me think of one of the ways we know we are living the Christian life the way it is supposed to be lived, and that's persecution. When we choose to live for Christ—or "fly over the right target," as my friend put it—we *will* be shot at.

For the most part, wearing the label "Christian" is acceptable in our culture. But that acceptability ends when our faith actually makes a difference in how we live and talk, when we have the nerve to live righteously before the world. Jesus gave us words of encouragement in the area of suffering on His behalf:

> *Blessed are those who have been persecuted for the sake of righteousness, for theirs is the kingdom of heaven. Blessed are you when people insult you and persecute you, and falsely say all kinds of evil against you because of Me. Rejoice and be glad, for your reward in heaven is great; for in the same way they persecuted the prophets who were before you.* (Matthew 5:10–12)

As flesh-and-blood human beings, it's hard to think of being insulted, persecuted, slandered, and mistreated in terms of "blessing." Deciding to go in a direction that the majority is not willing to go will cause others to see you as "different," to put it mildly. That's because your life is a reminder of what others' lives should be but aren't. So, Jesus tells us, don't despair when you are persecuted, because when you suffer for the sake of righteousness you are in very good company.

That company includes a host of prophets who have gone before us—great men and women of God through the ages who endured persecution and received their rewards. This distinguished company also includes Jesus Himself, who, though He was completely innocent of any wrongdoing, was persecuted to the point of being hung on a cross to die a humiliating, agonizing death on our behalf.

Have you ever felt like you were being shot at simply because you have taken a stand for Christ? You might feel the same as a man I know whose family disowned him because he converted from Islam to follow Christ. Or maybe you feel like a friend of mine who was fired from his job because he refused to doctor up the sales report—basically to lie—to make his manager look good. Or maybe you can relate to public high school students who are hassled because of their desire to follow the Lord.

Remember, everyone who stands up for Christ will be persecuted in one way or another. But when we are persecuted we can see it as a blessing. None of us in our right minds would hold up a sign that says "Please persecute me." Nobody enjoys being ridiculed, mocked, or abused. But when that happens as a result of our stand for Jesus Christ, we can take heart. We must be doing something right!

HERE'S WHAT I WANT YOU TO REMEMBER TODAY:

Persecution can be seen as a blessing, as it shows us we're making a stand for Christ.

TRUTH BE TOLD . . .

I know a man who lived a lie for years. He was a masterful liar. He lied about his background, his education, his experiences. He even lied about his Christian testimony. What was even more disheartening is that he was on staff with a Christian organization. But the truth came out eventually. Through a chain of events, this man's lies toppled like a house of cards.

A lot of people would find that their lives are a lot less complicated if they'd just be truthful!

Whenever my father heard something that sounded wrong or dishonest, he would say, "You know, that doesn't sound right. But I'll tell you what, time tells no lie." In other words, it's only a matter of time until your lies catch up with you.

That was Jesus' point when He spoke these words:

But there is nothing covered up that will not be revealed, and hidden that will not be known. Accordingly, whatever you have said in the dark will be heard in the light, and what you have whispered in the inner rooms will be proclaimed upon the housetops. (Luke 12:2–3)

Jesus was saying that it's always better speak the truth, because it is the right thing to do and because the truth will eventually come out. Lies will be found uncovered, hypocrisy exposed. So, as one old sage put it, if you always tell the truth you never have to remember what you said.

This falls under the law of sowing and reaping, which says that you will receive the consequences for the things you do. We won't get away with anything, and that includes speaking untruthfully. There will be a day of reckoning for our actions, good and bad. Sometimes that day is in this life, sometimes in the next.

Everyone will answer for how he spoke and whether his words were completely truthful. In light of that, we need to make sure our words and actions are 100 percent true. As those who serve the living God, we should speak the truth, the whole truth, and nothing but the truth!

Not only must our words be honest and true, but our lives should also be reflections of those words. For example, if we say it's wrong to steal, then we need to make sure all our business dealings are handled completely honestly. If we say it's wrong to commit sexual sin, then we need to make sure we are pure in our thoughts and actions. In other words, we should do what we say.

Jesus' words in Luke 12 grabbed my heart. They say to me, "Crawford, make sure you are truthful in your speech and in your actions." Another way to put that is "Make sure you are never hypocritical in any area of your life."

I never want to dishonor my God by being dishonest in any way. And when I stand before Him on Judgment Day, I want to have a clear conscience, knowing that with His help, I was honest in my words and in my actions.

Speaking the truth: It's the right thing to do and the best way to deal with those around us. It's also the easiest way to live!

HERE'S WHAT I WANT YOU TO REMEMBER TODAY:

A clean conscience comes from a clean, truthful heart.

AN UNSHAKABLE FAITH

I played golf recently with a man whose company I really enjoyed. He was a funny person who also had a very serious, honest way about him. He told me some things about his extreme disappointment in Christianity.

My friend told me that he wasn't a Christian, but that he had been an active church member for years. He had also followed and observed some well-known Christian personalities, and when some of those people fell into immorality and disgrace, he became disheartened with the church and with, as he put it, the "Christian thing."

My friend's problem wasn't with Jesus Himself or with the Christian faith. What turned him off was the hypocrisy he saw within certain Christian circles. He told me he was putting his relationship with God on hold until he saw some authentic Christians.

I couldn't argue with his point about hypocrisy in the Christian community. Tragically, far too many of God's representatives are messing up for all the world to see. And I'm not just talking about those in leadership roles, either. I believe this is a problem that reaches all the way down to what I would call the "Sunday Christians."

But I had to challenge him about the conclusion it led him to: "You mean to tell me you walked away from God because of a couple of His messed-up representatives? What was the object of your faith? Was it people or Jesus Christ?"

That's a question each of us has to ask ourselves. What is the object of our faith? Is my faith based on the people or events around me? Or is it completely grounded in the Lord Jesus Christ? Jesus had some very pointed things to say about the foundation of faith we build our lives upon:

Why do you call Me, "Lord, Lord," and do not do what I say? Everyone who comes to Me and hears My words and acts on them, I will show you whom he is like: he is like a man building a house, who dug deep and laid a foundation on the rock; and when a flood occurred, the torrent burst against that house and could not shake it, because it had been well built. But the one who has heard and has not acted accordingly, is like a man who built a house on the ground without any foundation; and the torrent burst against it and immediately it collapsed, and the ruin of that house was great. (Luke 6:46–49)

Jesus likened our faith to the foundation of a house. When we put our faith in anything other than Christ, then the foundation will shake and that house will collapse under the pressures this life is certain to bring. However, when we place our faith firmly in Him, He says, the house will be well grounded, and nothing—not the cares of this world, not temptations, not the failings of those around us—will shake it.

Humans and human organizations can and will fail us, but Jesus will always remain faithful to His Word. We will have a victorious walk with Christ when we make sure that our faith is in Him and not in leaders or organizations of the faith.

HERE'S WHAT I WANT YOU TO REMEMBER TODAY:

Faith in anything or anyone but the person of the Lord Jesus Christ will let us down, but Jesus never will fail us.

PART 6

GO
AND MAKE
DISCIPLES

In the generations gone by He permitted all the nations to go their own ways; and yet He did not leave Himself without witness, in that He did good and gave you rains from heaven and fruitful seasons, satisfying your hearts with food and gladness.
—ACTS 14:16–17

OUR CALLING, OUR MISSION

IT'S ALL ABOUT THE PEOPLE

THE TESTIMONY OF TRANSFORMATION

THE URGENCY OF THE TIME

STAYING IN OUR PLACE

SEEING PAST THE DIFFERENCES

FOXHOLE FAITH

HANGING OUT WITH SINNERS

OUR CALLING, OUR MISSION

When I was seventeen, I got a summer job at a factory that made prefabricated houses. I was really excited about that because back in those days a lot of money could be made in that business, and I was going to be earning more than I had ever made before. I thought that by the end of the summer my pockets would be stuffed.

I showed up my first day ready and willing to go, but there was a problem. My supervisor barely communicated with me. The first couple of weeks I was on the job, he never told me what he expected of me. I had no idea whether I was doing what my boss wanted. Then one day, three weeks after I started, my boss told me I wasn't doing the job and fired me. I'm not saying I was totally without blame in this situation. I should have been more aggressive in finding out my assignment. The bottom line is that this was a painful learning experience for me.

Although earthly bosses may not always communicate clearly what we are to be doing, our "Boss" in heaven has very clearly spelled out our mission on earth. In Matthew 28, Jesus gave us our job description. In this passage, our resurrected Lord was speaking to His disciples when He spoke these words: "Go therefore and make disciples of all the nations, baptizing them in the name of the Father and the Son and the Holy Spirit" (v. 19).

This single command is the essence of our mission as followers of Jesus Christ this side of heaven. But what does it mean to go? Does it mean each and every believer is called to serve on the foreign mission field? Read on!

When Jesus said "Go therefore," He used what is called a circumstantial participle. In other words, that expression could have been translated "While you're going" or "As you're going."

Why is that distinction so important? Well, it means everything when it comes to our calling to make disciples. It means that the arenas for accomplishing God's stated mission for us aren't limited to foreign missions. We don't necessarily have to get on an airplane and travel to a foreign country in order to fulfill Jesus' calling.

In order to fulfill the mission God has placed before us, we need to understand what is expected of us, and it's simply this: We are to "make disciples" wherever we are and whatever we are doing. Whether we are at work or play, with friends or relatives, at home or away, we are to be ready to present the love, forgiveness, cleansing, and hope of Jesus Christ to those around us.

God expects us to affect people for Him. I believe that if we will just keep our eyes open and actively seek opportunities to "make disciples," God will bring into our lives those people who need Him and are ready to hear the gospel.

Whether you're going to work or attending school, whether you are cutting the grass in your front yard or going to the mall, you are right where God wants you to be in order to reach out and touch the world for Him.

It's a tremendous responsibility, but it's also a wonderful privilege!

HERE'S WHAT I WANT YOU TO REMEMBER TODAY:

God wants to use you right where you are to reach out and touch the world.

IT'S ALL ABOUT THE PEOPLE

I was in a hurry, and I didn't have time to deal with this person.

I had an appointment to talk to a very prominent Atlanta businessman about a joint venture we were involved in to reach hundreds of thousands of Atlantans with the gospel via a television special. This was important stuff!

The businessman was very busy and I was late. I didn't have much time, so I parked my car and hustled down the street toward his downtown office. As I neared the office, I became quite irritated when I saw a homeless man lying on the sidewalk, blocking the doorway. As I approached the man, thoughts of indignation—thoughts I believed at that moment to be justified, given my mission that day—crossed my mind.

Why doesn't he get a job? I thought. *There are shelters he can go to. I'd better be careful when I pass him. He might be dangerous.*

Now I was more frustrated than ever, and I stepped over the man on my way into the office building. I entered the front door and headed for the elevator. Once inside, it hit me. *That poor man is somebody's son,* I thought. *He might be somebody's father. And he was created in the image of God!*

The irony of what I had done landed hard on me. Here I was, getting ready to sit down in a conference room to talk with a businessman about reaching the city of Atlanta for Christ, yet my heart was cold and callused toward this needy man. I was so caught up in my "ministry" that I literally stepped over a man Jesus died to save.

I wonder how many of us are so caught up in our ministries and activities that we forget that we are put here to love those whom Jesus came to save? I'm not suggesting that the tasks we perform and ministries we carry out aren't important. But, as 1 Corinthians 13 tells us, if we do those things and don't have love for those Christ came to save, we are wasting our time.

Jesus was the ultimate example of love in action. He showed us what it means to lovingly reach out to people. Matthew captured a beautiful picture of our Lord doing just that:

> *Jesus was going through all the cities and villages, teaching in their synagogues and proclaiming the gospel of the kingdom, and healing every kind of disease and every kind of sickness.* (Matthew 9:35)

Matthew went on in the next verse to define Jesus' motivation for His actions: "Seeing the people, *He felt compassion* for them, because they were distressed and dispirited like sheep without a shepherd" (Matthew 9:36, italics added).

"Seeing . . . He felt." Not "Seeing . . . He organized" or "Seeing . . . He analyzed." Jesus acted on these people's behalf because of His compassionate love for them.

What do you feel when you see the condition of fallen humanity? When you see the young people in our streets doing things to ruin their lives? When you see families falling apart because of alcohol?

Ask yourself, What do I really feel for people such as these? But more important, ask yourself if you are ready to put actions behind your feelings.

HERE'S WHAT I WANT YOU TO REMEMBER TODAY:
—◦◦◦—

Christ died for people, not for our activities or ministry organizations. Search your heart and ask yourself how important people—lost and dying people who were created in God's image—really are to you.

THE TESTIMONY OF TRANSFORMATION

I have a friend who pastors an exciting church in inner-city Atlanta. Joe Cobb ministers powerfully to the poor and disenfranchised and to those who have succumbed to alcoholism, drug addiction, and other life-shattering problems.

Joe is effective in his ministry for two reasons. The first reason is, frankly, that he has "been there." Before he came to Christ, Joe's life was a wreck in every way. He knows what it means to be looked down upon. He understands what it's like to be controlled by drugs and alcohol. He empathizes with those who have to hustle just to get by. He knows what it means to be empty and looking for love.

The second, and more important, reason for Joe's effectiveness in ministry is that God has transformed him and made him what he is today. At one time, Joe's life looked hopeless. But Jesus came into his life and dramatically transformed him. The healing, restorative power of Christ dramatically transformed this man.

At first, those who knew Joe were skeptical of his conversion, but it wasn't long before the reality of his changed life convinced people around him that what had happened to him was real. Soon people were drawn to him and his ministry.

There's no better testimony than real transformation, no better witness than a truly changed life.

Sometimes we can forget that the gospel is not just a bunch of words but the very power of God to heal, transform, and save through the blood of the Lord Jesus Christ. Sadly, we tend to reduce the gospel to nothing more than a verbal presentation.

The gospel of John contains an account of one woman who knew personally of the power of Jesus Christ to transform lives.

Here is the story of the Samaritan woman's testimony to those around her:

> *From that city many of the Samaritans believed in Him because of the word of the woman who testified, "He told me all the things that I have done." So when the Samaritans came to Jesus, they were asking Him to stay with them; and He stayed there two days. Many more believed because of His word; and they were saying to the woman, "It is no longer because of what you said that we believe, for we have heard for ourselves and know that this One is indeed the Savior of the world."* (John 4:39–42)

Her encounter with Jesus changed the Samaritan woman's life powerfully, and her testimony drew others toward the Savior. It wasn't just the words she spoke about that encounter but the enthusiasm with which she witnessed of the power of Christ in her life.

We need to make sure that we are theologically accurate in our presentation of the gospel, but we also need to make sure we live it out before those around us. When we tell others the gospel, it's the reality of what Jesus has done for us that brings authenticity to the message.

Preach the gospel to the world around you, using the words of your mouth. But always remember to shine for the reality of God's love by allowing people to see the way Christ has transformed you.

HERE'S WHAT I WANT YOU TO REMEMBER TODAY:

People can argue with your words, no matter how true they are. What they can't argue with are the results the gospel has had in your life.

THE URGENCY OF THE TIME

My youngest daughter, Holly, recently told me about a discussion she had with some of her friends on the subject of hell. She said that while they were talking about the sufferings and finality of hell, it struck her that when death comes there are no more opportunities to come to Christ.

As she ended her remarks and observations I said to her, "That's right, sweetheart, and that's why Dad does what he does and that's why your brother Bryan does what he does."

As Christians, we need to lay hold of the finality of death and the certainty of hell for those who haven't come to Jesus Christ. We need to realize how important it is to tell others the gospel right now, because when this life is over, there really are no more chances to turn to Christ.

I want you to think about something. Maybe you know someone right now who needs to hear the message of salvation through Jesus Christ. You've been thinking about telling the person, and maybe you've even rehearsed what you are going to say.

"I'll get around to it one day," you tell yourself. "When the time is right, I'll tell this person about Jesus. I don't want to seem pushy, so I'll wait for the subject of God to come up. Then I'll let them know about how they need Jesus."

There's a problem with that way of thinking, and it's the same problem the person has who believes he or she has time to surrender to Christ. It's the problem of uncertainty. None of us knows what tomorrow brings. For that matter, we aren't even guaranteed a tomorrow!

There is one guarantee in this life, and it's the love of God that reached out to us in the person of Jesus Christ. Beyond that, we aren't guaranteed one more moment of life on this earth. And when this life is over, that's it. Then it's time to face a God whose only question to us will be, "What did you do with My Son?"

Near the end of Jesus' earthly ministry—just before He went to the cross—the people who followed Jesus and heard His message of hope daily had one more chance to hear His plea: "And Jesus cried out and said, 'He who believes in Me, does not believe in Me but in Him who sent Me'" (John 12:44).

Jesus understood the urgency of the times. This impassioned cry was to give the people one more chance to hear Him tell them that believing in Jesus Christ was the same as believing in the Father who sent Him.

God gives us opportunities to tell others about salvation through Jesus Christ, but we need to understand the urgency of the times we are in. Right now, you may be thinking of a friend, a neighbor, a coworker, or a family member who needs Jesus. It's time for you to put aside your human pride and fear and tell that person the Good News. You have the opportunity, so it's time to move!

We need to stop procrastinating and move out in obedience to God's call to reach those around us for Him.

HERE'S WHAT I WANT YOU TO REMEMBER TODAY:

When someone's life ends, so do that person's opportunities to turn to Christ. Make sure those you love know what it takes to receive salvation.

STAYING IN OUR PLACE

My youngest son called me from college recently to talk to me about a burden he had. He had been discussing the gospel with a man, but the results were not what he had hoped for. Time and time again, my son sought the man out to tell him the Good News. But the man did not respond positively. I could tell that Bryndan was discouraged, so I asked him about it.

"Son, are you down about this?" I asked. "Are you disappointed?"

"Yeah, Dad, I really am," he said. "For whatever reason, God has given me a real love for this young man, and I want to see him come into the kingdom."

"Son, you have to remember that God loves him more than you do," I reminded Bryndan. "You can't make him come to Christ. Only God can do that."

"Yeah, I know," he said. "I guess I had sort of forgotten about that."

Then I encouraged Bryndan to keep up the good work: "Son, the only thing you need to do is to be faithful in sharing the gospel. Trust God to do His work. You may be one link in a long chain of events that God will use one day to finally turn the lights on in this man's heart and mind, and he'll turn from his sin and respond to Christ."

I prayed with Bryndan over the phone, said good night, then hung up. I sat back and thought about our conversation. I realized that Bryndan had done the same thing so many well-meaning Christians do: take responsibility for someone else's response to a presentation of the gospel.

I think it's easy for us to forget our role in bringing people to Christ. We tend to think that it's our job to use logic, reason, and slick communication to "persuade" someone to come to the Savior. Although it is important for us to be ready to clearly present the gospel in creative and engaging ways, we need to remember that only the Holy Spirit can touch a person's heart and bring that person to salvation.

Jesus told the disciples that it would be the Holy Spirit's job to touch people's hearts and convict them of sin and their need for the Savior:

> *But I tell you the truth, it is to your advantage that I go away; for if I do not go away, the Helper will not come to you; but if I go, I will send Him to you. And He, when He comes, will convict the world concerning sin and righteousness and judgment.* (John 16:7–8)

If I had my way, everyone I talk to about Jesus would bend the knee and surrender to Him on the spot. But I have to remind myself that I can't allow my own expectations or goals to become the criteria for success in my witness for Jesus Christ.

Jesus charged us with the task of preaching the gospel to the world around us. We are to be faithful in that calling. We are to pour ourselves wholeheartedly into seeing that those around us hear the gospel. But we need to remember always that only God can turn a heart toward Him.

HERE'S WHAT I WANT YOU TO REMEMBER TODAY:

As you tell the Good News, rest and rely on the Holy Spirit. Place the results in God's hands and leave them there!

SEEING PAST THE DIFFERENCES

Sometimes our greatest life experiences spring from the most awkward of moments. I know that is true for me. In the fall of 1968, I left home and went off to a Christian college. Excited and apprehensive about my living arrangement, I waltzed into the dorm room, where I first met my new roommate, a young white man named Bill.

Bill and I will both admit that there was initially some awkwardness, even skepticism, between us. Our difference wasn't just the color of our skin. Our backgrounds were also completely different. Bill came from a white suburban community, while I grew up in the predominantly black central part of Newark, New Jersey.

It was a great experience for both of us. I hadn't been around a lot of white folks, and Bill hadn't personally known many blacks. But we both learned a great deal about looking past differences such as skin color and background to see the real person. We learned that although all Christians are different, they are bound together by the love of Jesus.

By the way, in time Bill became the best friend I ever had. Bill and I were the best men at each other's weddings, and we've greatly influenced each other's families and ministries. I believe that I'm doing what I'm doing today largely due to Bill's influence on my life.

Bill and I don't see each other now in terms of our skin color; rather, we see each other as friends and brothers in the Lord Jesus Christ. God used Bill to help me to think beyond my own cultural boundaries and to realize that the Great

Commission of our Savior is never to be influenced by skin color or cultural differences.

Jesus Christ has commissioned us to make a difference in all of society. It's not just a nice thing we do as Christians. When Jesus said, "Go therefore and make disciples of all the nations" (Matthew 28:19), it was a command and part of the Great Commission to win others to Him.

In this context, the word *nations* can be translated "ethnicities" or "peoples." In other words, Jesus has commanded us to reach out to *all* ethnicities and peoples of the world—those in our own communities and those in other parts of the world.

In Acts 1:8 Jesus said, "You will receive power when the Holy Spirit has come upon you; and you shall be My witnesses both in Jerusalem, and in all Judea and Samaria, and even to the remotest part of the earth."

I think we often misapply that verse when it comes to forming strategies for reaching others for Jesus. We think it means reaching our part of the world first, then moving out into other parts of the world. But a close examination of this verse underscores what Jesus said in Matthew 28:19. In that verse, Jesus used the words "both in." I believe this means that at the same time we're reaching people who are "like us," we ought to be reaching people who are different from us—in their skin color, in their culture, in their thinking.

That's the heart of God!

HERE'S WHAT I WANT YOU TO REMEMBER TODAY:

Christ died for the whole world—for people of all colors, cultures, and backgrounds—and His offer of salvation is to the whole world.

FOXHOLE FAITH

I have a friend who saw a lot of combat in the Vietnam War. In fact, he was severely wounded in action and also highly decorated for his valor. I asked this man one time what it felt like to constantly be in harm's way, to be literally under fire when you are nineteen or twenty years old.

"You are scared to death most of the time, and you realized that you needed each other, so you tended to focus on what was really important and you watched each other's backs," he said. "Under pressure, under those dangerous circumstances, you realize that you hold each other's lives literally in your hands."

My friend also gave great credence to the old saying that there are no atheists in foxholes: "Guys prayed who would otherwise never even mention God's name—at least not in a decent way—let alone talk to Him," he said.

I think it would do the church some good to realize that we are in as desperate and dangerous a situation as those men who fought in the Vietnam War. No, we aren't necessarily in danger of dying any minute. But millions of people around us are in grave danger of perishing eternally, and their lives are being shattered and destroyed by sin.

I don't think we take this danger seriously enough. We don't live as if people we come in contact with could enter into a Christless eternity, or as if Jesus could return at any time, leaving behind people we should be working to bring to Him.

God's work isn't just something we do "on the fly." It's not some kind of recreation or play for us, and it's not some kind of earthly profession we enter into. Yes, we can actually enjoy taking Jesus to people around us, and yes, we need to take that work very seriously. But it's not about man's results, but about God breaking through on our behalf. It's about us realizing that apart from God's intervention, we can do nothing for Him. It's about realizing that not one soul will turn to Him unless He draws that person.

The early disciples were seized with this sense of urgency and dependence on God. In the first chapter of Acts, we read of early believers who saw the task before them and who knew where to turn to see that task through: "These all with one mind were continually devoting themselves to prayer, along with the women, and Mary the mother of Jesus, and with His brothers" (Acts 1:14).

This takes place in a context of extreme urgency. Jesus had just ascended to heaven, and the people knew of the challenges that lay ahead. These followers of Christ knew they needed a spirit of unity and persistent prayer in order to carry out the instructions the Master had just given them.

We should ask God to give us that same sense of urgency. We should ask Him to reveal to us the nature of the war that is going on around us. We need hearts filled with compassion for the casualties of this war, hearts that are willing to watch the backs of those who stand, tend to the wounded, and give comfort to those who are frightened.

HERE'S WHAT I WANT YOU TO REMEMBER TODAY:

We need to grasp just how desperate a situation the world around is in, then ask God to move on our behalf to reach those we reach out to for Him.

HANGING OUT WITH SINNERS

I'm a great believer in Bible education. I am a graduate of one Bible college and am now on the board of directors of another. My older son graduated from Bible school, and my younger son is presently attending one.

Bible colleges do a great job giving students a solid foundation in understanding Scripture and in forming a positive biblical worldview. But there is a challenge facing these schools, and it's the isolation that can be a part of the college experience. In a Bible college, the student is inundated with biblical teaching, and it can be easy, if the student isn't careful, to lose contact with the outside world, to become isolated from those we are called to reach: sinners.

I believe that problem isn't limited to Bible colleges, either. I think there is a bit of a bunker mentality within the church as a whole. There is something of an us-versus-them way of thinking, where we see the world outside as an enemy to be defeated instead of reached for Jesus Christ. We have created for ourselves safe havens of ministry, where we reduce ministry to discussing the truths of God among ourselves. We treat our churches as ministry centers that people must come to so they can hear the Good News, rather than as training grounds to equip us to go out and reach the world for Jesus.

Our job as followers of Jesus Christ is to associate with the lost, to hang out with sinners so that we can tell them about and show them God's love. Jesus not only commanded us to do that; He did it Himself, often in the face of opposition from religious leaders:

And Levi gave a big reception for Him in his house; and there was a great crowd of tax collectors and other people who were reclining at the table with them. The Pharisees and their scribes began grumbling at His disciples, saying, "Why do you eat and drink with the tax collectors and sinners?" And Jesus answered and said to them, "It is not those who are well who need a physician, but those who are sick. I have not come to call the righteous but sinners to repentance."
(Luke 5:29–32)

We are to follow the example of our Lord, who came not simply to spend all His time with religious leaders or teachers of the law. He came to reach out to those who were lost, to heal those who were sick, and to call to repentance those who were lost in sin. In order to do that, Jesus went out of His way to spend time in the presence of sinners.

He calls us to do the very same thing.

We live in a world full of seriously lost people. Their lives are being destroyed by sin, and they desperately need to hear the message of the gospel of Christ. When we get up from our church pews on Sunday or our Bible studies on Wednesday, we need to get out there and spend time with them.

HERE'S WHAT I WANT YOU TO REMEMBER TODAY:

You won't make a difference in the lives of lost sinners until you make an effort to get out there and associate with these people.

PART 7

GOD'S FAITHFUL PROVISION

And the Lord will continually guide you,
And satisfy your desire in scorched places,
And give strength to your bones;
And you will be like a watered garden,
And like a spring of water whose waters do not fail.
—ISAIAH 58:11

RECEIVING WISDOM

Once when he was in college, my oldest son Bryan had a fairly serious financial need. Now, he's had needs before—a pair of shoes here, or book money there—but this time he was in trouble and he needed help.

What made this situation really unusual is that Bryan's mother and I knew nothing about it. Bryan usually spoke up when he needed something, but this time he said nothing. I didn't find out about his problems until later, and when I did, I had to ask him why he didn't come to me for help.

"Bryan, why didn't you tell us you had a need?" I asked. "We love you, son, and we would have tried to help you meet that need."

"Dad, I just didn't want to bother you and Mom," he answered. "I wanted to trust God myself for this one."

As a father who is also a Christian man, I had mixed feelings about that. On one hand, I was proud that Bryan wanted to trust God to meet his needs. On the other hand, I'm his father, and I see it as part of my God-given responsibility as Dad to do all I can to meet my children's needs.

When I think about that time in my son's life, I can't help but compare how I felt with how I think God must feel when we don't go to Him with our most fundamental needs. God, our loving heavenly Father, promises to meet our earthly needs, if we just approach Him and ask.

As human beings with limited understanding, I believe one of our greatest needs in this earthly life is wisdom. We face so many situations—in our interpersonal relationships, in our-ministries, in our financial lives—that must be handled skill-fully, practically, and appropriately. To do that we need the wisdom only God can give us.

James had something to say to those who recognized their need for wisdom:

But if any of you lacks wisdom, let him ask of God, who gives to all generously and without reproach, and it will be given to him. But he must ask in faith without any doubting, for the one who doubts is like the surf of the sea, driven and tossed by the wind. For that man ought not expect that he will receive anything from the Lord, being a double-minded man, unstable in all his ways. (James 1:5–8)

This is what is called a conditional promise. This passage assures us that when we go to God and ask for wisdom, God doesn't sit up in heaven rolling His eyes at how naive and ignorant we are. No, He happily gives us the wisdom we need, and it's a wisdom that far surpasses our own. The condition in this promise is that we must come to God in faith, believing that He wants to give us what we need. Without that faith, we are warned, we can expect to receive nothing from God.

Do you need wisdom—the wisdom of God? Does life have you in a place where your own wisdom just isn't going to cut it? Then go to God, and He will give you what you need!

HERE'S WHAT I WANT YOU TO REMEMBER TODAY:

You don't have to be stuck with question marks. If you need wisdom, ask for it, and God will give freely.

TRUSTING THE HEALER

Frank Merry is a friend of mine who is now in heaven. He died of cancer a few years ago. I miss Frank, but I look forward to the day when I will see my friend in his glorified body.

When Frank announced that he had cancer, some of his friends called him and sent him e-mails, letters, and notes to tell him they were trusting God for Frank's miraculous healing here on earth. They were just sure Frank's body would be cleansed and healed of the cancer.

Those who know Frank well know he was a wonderfully balanced man. I had a conversation with Frank during his illness, and we talked about what people were saying about his healing. What he told me was classic. He said, "I'm trusting the Healer, not the healing."

This was not at all to say that Frank didn't believe God could heal him. He believed that God has the power to heal, but that the healing would only take place if it were to further His own purposes for Frank's life.

"God can do whatever He wants to do with me," Frank said. "I have prayed for my own personal healing this side of heaven, but I know that God has purposes beyond me. He has purposes beyond my desires, so I have committed myself completely to Him, and whatever He decides to do is all right with me."

I don't want to criticize anyone, but sometimes when I watch or listen to some Christian television and radio programming, I wonder if there isn't a tendency on the part of some to elevate what God *does* above who He *is*. In other words, maybe some are looking at the healing before they look at the Healer.

A lot of Christians may be guilty of putting God on trial, albeit in a very subtle way. We may look for some "miracle," but when it doesn't come we are disappointed in God. Oh, we still believe in Him and in Christ's power to save, but in a way we wonder if God didn't fall short for us.

Jesus addressed this issue directly in the gospel of John when He chided those who followed Him for their lack of faith. A royal official approached Jesus and asked Him to heal his sick son. Jesus said to him, "Unless you people see signs and wonders, you simply will not believe" (John 4:48).

Jesus, in effect, was asking these people, "How much more do I have to do before you believe Me? You want more signs and wonders and healing, but are you trusting in those things and not in Me?"

Jesus did perform a miracle that day, healing the official's son. So His point was not that we can't glorify and praise God when He does something spectacular. His point was that God can do whatever He wants, any way He wants to do it, but our worship and affection must be targeted toward Him and not the spectacular things He does.

God is at work in the lives of His people every moment, even if there isn't some spectacular sign or wonder. He provides for us all that we need. We need to be careful that we don't place our faith on what God does instead of who He is.

HERE'S WHAT I WANT YOU TO REMEMBER TODAY:

It's OK to pray for miracles, but our faith must be in the One who performs them, not the miracles themselves.

APPROACHING GOD—WITH AN OPEN HAND

A number of years ago I spoke at a conference in Manila in the Philippines. Each morning as I left my hotel to walk the short distance to the conference center, I felt as though my heart was being torn from my chest. During that short walk, I passed countless homeless people, beggars sitting by the side of the road.

I'll never forget the sorrow I felt as I passed by those people, those precious souls with so little hope. But one image from that trip was burned deeply and permanently into my heart and mind. It was a woman sitting on the sidewalk. In one hand she clutched her baby, and she held out the other hand to passers-by in hopes that someone would give her some money so she could feed herself and her infant.

There's no way I could have walked by this scene and not been touched deeply by how incredibly needy these people were. Amazingly, though, God used this scene to remind me of someone who in some ways was every bit as destitute: me.

When I think of that scene, it's almost as if God is saying to me, "Crawford, that's the way I want you to be. I want you to remember how needy you are and stretch out your hand to Me and let Me meet your needs."

Jesus said in Matthew chapter 5 verse 3 at the very beginning of what we call the Beatitudes, "Blessed are the poor in spirit, for theirs is the kingdom of heaven." It's one of the great paradoxes of the Christian faith: We can only realize the wealth we have in Christ when we understand how personally impoverished we are. I believe that's at the heart of Jesus' words in Revelation 3:17–18:

Because you say, "I am rich, and have become wealthy, and have need of nothing," and you do not know that you are wretched and miserable and poor and blind and naked, I advise you to buy from Me gold refined by fire so that you may become rich, and white garments so that you may clothe yourself.

One of the great problems we have with Christianity in this culture is that we're too impressed with ourselves. We have all the trappings, all the trinkets of "rich religion." We see ourselves as blessings to God, as having so much to offer Him that He couldn't help but reach down and save us for Himself. We forget that apart from God, apart from what He has done for us, we have nothing and we are nothing. We lose sight of the fact that there is nothing about us that commends us to God. We forget that we are a needy people who need to approach God with praises in our mouths and empty hands stretched toward Him.

We are closest to God when we embrace the fact that we are God-dependent beggars with nothing to offer Him but an empty, outstretched hand. Apart from Him we are completely destitute and empty. We must approach God with one hand holding out our need and the other outstretched in praise for Him for His wonderful provision of the inheritance of the kingdom of God.

HERE'S WHAT I WANT YOU TO REMEMBER TODAY:

God has given us our inheritance because we are needy, impoverished people. Let's not forget that we are God-dependent beggars.

HE'S GOT YOU COVERED

I recently took my ten-year-old nephew J. J. on a speaking engagement. He was overwhelmed when we got there. It was a huge auditorium, thousands of people were there, and television cameras were everywhere.

It made me smile to see J. J.'s reaction to everything, but after a while he asked me a question that made me chuckle. He looked at me and, with a look of concern on his face, he said, "Uncle C. W., do I need some money for food?"

"No, buddy," I said with a smile. "You don't need anything. The folks here have taken care of everything. As long as you're with me you don't have need for anything."

God must look down on us and shake His head when He sees us wringing our hands and wondering if we will have what we need to live a life that pleases Him. I believe He would say the same thing I said to J. J.: "As long as you're with Me, you don't have need for anything."

It's a truth we can take from the written Word of God: He has us covered! The apostle Paul addressed this issue when he wrote, "Now to Him who is able to do far more abundantly beyond all that we ask or think, according to the power that works within us, to Him be the glory in the church and in Christ Jesus" (Ephesians 3:20–21).

What an amazing promise! This means that the same power that raised Jesus Christ from the dead rests within us, ready to enable us to rise to any challenge we may face. No matter what task is ahead, no matter what problem lies before you, God has promised that the power that lives within us through the Spirit of God is more than enough for us to emerge victorious.

In this verse, the verb *works* is in the present tense, meaning that God did not just do the work in us at the time we first received salvation, but continues to work within us. That's right! God's power is at work in you at this very moment.

I want to highlight three ways that power works within us. The first is His conforming us to the image of His Son, meaning He is working within us to make us more like Jesus. God uses the problems we face in this life, combined with the power of His Spirit, to change us and make us into reflections of Christ.

The second way that power works within us is by enabling us to do that which, in our own efforts, is impossible. For example, that power enables us to overcome even the most stubborn habitual sin, and it enables us to speak with authority to others about the Lord Jesus Christ.

Third, that power is at work to sustain us. We all go through times of trouble and trial, times when we don't know what we are going to do next. The power of God works within us during those times to keep us and give us balance.

My friend Joseph Garlington likes to say, "God's power is getting you ready for what He already has ready for you." Another way to say that is, no matter what your needs are, no matter how desperate a situation God is taking you through, you will have the power to be victorious.

Always remember, He's got you covered!

HERE'S WHAT I WANT YOU TO REMEMBER TODAY:

It's a simple but profound truth: God supplies us everything we need by giving us the power of His Spirit.

A HAND OF PROVISION

My wife, Karen, and I have been married thirty wonderful years, but we both remember well our first year of marriage. It was a wonderful time of learning some great lessons about God's provision.

One stretch during that first year, we were extremely low on money—so low, in fact, that we didn't have enough to last us the rest of the month. To make matters worse, we were out of food.

I guess you could say God had us where He wanted us.

One day, we paid my parents a visit. We didn't say anything about our needs, and as far as I know, there was no way they could have known about them. But as we were getting ready to leave, Mom said, "Oh, by the way, your dad bought a side of beef, and we've got more in the freezer than we can handle. Karen, why don't you go downstairs and fill a couple of shopping bags with the meat and take it home."

There it was. Out of nowhere, we had enough meat to last us for a month.

God, once again You came through, I thought.

An old line says, "Jesus is never early, and He's never late. He's always right on time." Karen and I have learned that as we've seen God faithfully provide for us through the years. I can't tell you how many times God has stepped in just in the nick of time and intervened on our behalf. So many times it has seemed that we were in dire straits, and then God stepped in and met us at our point of greatest need.

God always comes through! An account in the gospel of John illustrates this point perfectly. The text tells us that at certain seasons an angel stirred up the water in a particular pool, and the first sick person to get in the pool was healed. It continues:

A man was there who had been ill for thirty-eight years. When Jesus saw him lying there, and knew that he had already been a long time in that condition, He said to him, "Do you wish to get well?" The sick man answered Him, "Sir, I have no man to put me into the pool when the water is stirred up, but while I am coming, another steps down before me." Jesus said to him, "Get up, pick up your pallet and walk." Immediately the man became well, and picked up his pallet and began to walk. (John 5:5–9)

I want to point out something I think we sometimes miss in this story. This man was at the pool because there was healing power in the water—*if* you could get into the water. But when Jesus showed up, the man no longer needed to get in the pool because Jesus reached out and healed him on the spot.

At just the right time, Jesus met this man's needs, but He did it in a way the man didn't expect. I think the man expected Jesus to reach down and help him into the water. Instead, Jesus simply told him to get up, because he was healed.

Jesus knows our needs, and He wants to meet those needs. All we need to do is ask Him, trust Him, and stand back and watch Him work—in His way and in His timing.

HERE'S WHAT I WANT YOU TO REMEMBER TODAY:

God always meets our needs, in the best way and in the right timing. We need to remember that His ways are not our ways, and His timing is not our timing.

HE MEETS OUR NEEDS—AND THEN SOME

I recently took a trip to visit our younger son, who is a freshman in college. It was a great time for both of us. I hadn't seen him in several months, and we had a lot of catching up to do. We talked about class, his social life, and his walk with the Lord. For the first time, it was as if we were talking man to man. Eventually, however, the "dad" in me came out, and I had to find out if my boy had some needs I could meet.

"Son, do you need anything at all?" I asked.

"Well, Dad," he said, "I do need a new pair of shoes."

I smiled at him and said, "Well, you caught me at just the right time. I happen to have a few extra shekels in my pocket. Let's hit the mall!"

We went to the mall, and I bought him the shoes he needed. I also bought him a few other things, including a couple of sweaters that he didn't really need but that I thought he should have.

It's hard to explain how it warms a father's heart to meet his children's needs. My wife and I have four children, and I have always been committed to meeting the needs of each and every one of them. It was never out of a sense of duty that I did those things, but out of my love for them and my desire to see them comfortable and happy.

I believe our heavenly Father approaches meeting our needs the same way. No, He doesn't always give us everything we want—from what I can see, that's a matter of His discretion—but He gives us everything we need.

King David started Psalm 23 by declaring, "The Lord is my

Shepherd, I shall not want." We can easily reword this verse to read, "The Lord is my Shepherd. I do not lack for anything" or "The Lord is my Shepherd. I have all that I need."

I think we need to remember that David didn't write this Psalm in the context of abundance. Most scholars believe he wrote this prior to the time that he was sitting on the throne. It was a lean time for David, and he lived a hand-to-mouth existence. But through all that, he learned that God alone was enough. God committed Himself to providing for David during the tough times, and He carried that commitment for the rest of his life.

You might have a special need today. Maybe you wonder if God is going to come through for you. It could be anything from a financial challenge to a health problem. I can assure you that God sees your need and that He will give you exactly what you need to face it.

We should rejoice in the fact that God, because of who He is, has taken us on as His responsibility. He will always meet our needs. We should feel especially blessed when our Father picks us up a couple of sweaters we don't really need.

HERE'S WHAT I WANT YOU TO REMEMBER TODAY:

God doesn't just meet our needs; He does so with a joyful heart. We can approach God boldly and confidently, knowing He wants to meet our needs.

DEVELOPING A GRATEFUL HEART

Have you noticed how easy it is to fall into ungratefulness, even when things are going well, when God's blessings are flowing at their fullest? I've always thought that the more we are blessed, the easier it is to start taking those blessings for granted. That's why several years ago I began doing something in my prayer life that has literally revolutionized my life.

Let me tell you about it. As part of my regular prayer life, I set aside every Tuesday as a day of thanksgiving. I don't ask God for anything those days—not for myself or for anyone else. I just spend my whole prayer time that day thanking God for every wonderful thing He has done for me. I thank Him for creating me, for saving me, for setting me aside for His service. I thank Him for my family, for my friends, and for keeping me healthy. I thank Him for anything and everything I can think of to be thankful for.

I've been amazed at the changes my day of thanks has made in my heart and mind. My entire perspective is changed as I set aside my needs and desires and focus on the greatness of God and how very good He has been to me. By the end of that day, my whole being sings praise to His wonderful, holy name.

King David was very much aware of God's favor and blessing on his life, and he expressed his gratitude in the Psalms: "You prepare a table before me in the presence of my enemies; You have anointed my head with oil; my cup overflows" (Psalm 23:5).

This is not a general "Thank You, God, for blessing me." It's stronger than that. David is praising God for His wonderful favor and love and for honoring him even before those who were his enemies. David is thanking and praising God for singling him out, for choosing him, and for showering him with blessing.

David expressed the gratefulness of a man who had received from God more than he deserved. It's the kind of gratitude we should show now for an awesome, wonderful, generous God who pours out on us blessings infinitely above what we have coming to us.

Do you want a transformation of your heart? Do you want a new appreciation for the God you serve? Set aside some time to express to Him your thanks for all He is and all He has done for you. Make it a point not to ask for anything for yourself or for anyone else. Just make it a time to say "Thank You." Take a few moments to sit and write down all the things you are grateful for. Thank Him for being the God He is. Thank Him for the beauty of the creation around you. Thank Him for your family and your friends. Thank Him for the physical and material blessings He's given you.

When you do these things, you will develop a heart of gratitude, a heart that appreciates and loves God just for being who He is.

Let me warn you, though: Start this kind of prayer and it could be habit-forming.

HERE'S WHAT I WANT YOU TO REMEMBER TODAY:

It's good to take your needs and the needs of others before your heavenly Father. But don't forget to set aside time to thank and praise Him for all He does for you.

HE'S GIVEN US THE MESSAGE

Several years ago two Christians who didn't know I was a believer approached me to witness to me. I was curious about their approach, so I asked them what I had to do in order to be saved. I was surprised to find that their answers were not very clear.

There was no doubt in my mind that these two people loved the Lord or that they had a heart for presenting His message. The problem, however, was that they didn't know the message well enough to communicate it clearly and concisely.

That experience taught me something I will never forget. It showed me that we believers can't assume that we will somehow automatically know what to say to people when we have a chance to tell the Good News of Christ's love. It showed me that we need to make use of the information God has provided us in His Word, as well as in other published materials.

We need to be passionate about communicating the gospel message to the lost people around us. We need to always keep in mind that men and women who do not come to Christ will be eternally lost, that they will wind up in hell, where they will stay forever. We need to ask the Holy Spirit to touch our hearts with a compassion for those who don't yet know Jesus Christ. And we need to live for the message that God has made a way for each and every one of us not only to avoid hell but to spend eternity with Him in heaven.

Along with our passion for the message, we need to make sure we can *communicate* the gospel in a way that not only is clear and concise, but that fits the audience we are trying to reach.

In the book of Acts is an account of the apostle Paul explaining to King Agrippa what he is communicating and his reason for communicating it:

So, having obtained help from God, I stand to this day testifying both to small and great, stating nothing but what the Prophets and Moses said was going to take place; that the Christ was to suffer, and that by reason of His resurrection from the dead He would be the first to proclaim light both to the Jewish people and to the Gentiles. (Acts 26:22–23)

In this passage, Paul set for us a great example of someone who was ready to communicate the message, even under severe fire. Even though Paul's life was on the line, he was able to look the king in the eye and say, in essence, "I must proclaim the message that Jesus Christ, the Son of God, came to this world, died on the cross for your sin, and rose from the dead to confirm that He was who He said He was."

We too can be prepared to present the message of Christ clearly and powerfully, because God has provided us with everything we need to be ready to do so. If you aren't sure you are ready to present the gospel clearly and concisely, then make use of the Word and other published material that is available to help you.

HERE'S WHAT I WANT YOU TO REMEMBER TODAY:

We must rely on the Holy Spirit to empower us to tell the Good News, but we must also know the message God has given us.

PART 8

A LIFE YIELDED TO GOD

"For the sons of Israel are My servants; they are My servants whom I brought out from the land of Egypt. I am the Lord your God."
—LEVITICUS 25:55

REMEMBER WHOSE YOU ARE

GOD'S RESPONSE TO PRIDE

LAYING IT ALL AT HIS FEET

THE HOLY SPIRIT'S ROLE

STAYING FOCUSED

RECEIVING FAVOR FROM GOD

GIVING GOD THE LEFTOVERS?

MAKING SOUND INVESTMENTS

YOUR CALLING, YOUR PASSION

REMEMBER WHOSE YOU ARE

My father used to tell my two sisters and me something when we were getting ready to leave the house: "Remember that your last name is Loritts."

In other words, "When you are outside the house, remember whom you represent."

My father taught my sisters and me his values and rules, and we knew what was expected of us when we were away from home—whether it was on a family vacation, a quick visit to friends or relatives, or a trip to the supermarket. We knew we would be in hot water with our father if our conduct was inconsistent with what he'd taught us from the time we were old enough to understand. We knew that we represented our father and that people saw a reflection of him in how we behaved.

My wife and I now have four wonderful children of our own, so I understand how important it was to my father that his children reflect who he was. I want my children to represent to the world around them the values Karen and I have instilled in them from the time they were babies. I want them to be representative of who I am as a father, as a man, and as one who follows Jesus Christ.

I can't help but believe that our heavenly Father would say something like that to those who are His. I am convinced that God wants us to remember whose we are as we live life in front of a watching world. It's been said that the only earthly glimpse of Jesus many people will see is through those who are His. I couldn't have said it better!

The apostle John gave us a description of what that glimpse

of Jesus looks like when he wrote, "This is the message we have heard from Him and announce to you, that God is Light, and in Him there is no darkness at all" (1 John 1:5).

John went on to tell us what a glimpse of Jesus *will not* look like: "If we say that we have fellowship [or partnership] with Him and yet walk in the darkness, we lie and do not practice the truth" (1 John 1:6).

In other words, how can you say that you're related to the Light while there's no light shining in your life? How can you say God is your Father, yet live as if you don't know Him?

Sadly, the world has a lot of professing Christians whose lives don't consistently and accurately reflect Jesus Christ. They are, as John put it, "walking in darkness." And those who walk in darkness can't reflect the light of God to a world that desperately needs to see a glimpse of Him.

I believe it's vitally important that we examine ourselves regularly to see that we are accurate reflections of our heavenly Father. We need to ask ourselves if people see Jesus in us. We need to honestly evaluate our behavior, attitudes, and actions to see that they present a true picture of Christ to the world around us.

If we find ourselves falling short in any of these areas, the Word promises us that if we confess our sins, God will forgive us and restore us. Then we truly will be representatives of our heavenly Father.

HERE'S WHAT I WANT YOU TO REMEMBER TODAY:

We need to be accurate reflections of the God we serve. When we are, we will glorify Him in all we do.

GOD'S RESPONSE TO PRIDE

Some of my fondest memories of when my kids were children were the times I took them to the park near our home so they could play on the playground there. The kids always had a great time, but to tell you the truth, I think I almost enjoyed going to the park more than they did.

Our girls were always pictures of reliance on their daddy. They liked to play it safe when we went to the park. They liked the swings, if they didn't go too high, and the teeter-totter—and only with Daddy there to keep an eye on them and make sure they didn't go too high or too fast.

The boys, however, liked to push the envelope when it came to playing in the park. Bryan and Bryndan wanted to go higher on the swings and faster on the merry-go-round. But I quickly found out that the boys had their limits.

There were two slides at the park we went to—one for the bigger kids and one for the little tykes. Every time we went to the park, we went through the same routine. I'd take the boys over to the small slide, but they always wanted to go to the big one.

"OK, let's go on the big sliding board," I would tell them, knowing what was about to happen. When I tried to help the boys up the ladder, their pride always kicked in: "No, Daddy!" they'd protest. "I can do it! I can do it!"

With their pride still in place after refusing my help, the boys would make their way up the ladder. That's when reality always set in. Every time they climbed to the top of that ladder, they'd look back down and see how high they were, panic, and cry out for help. Then I'd help them down and take them home.

Isn't it amazing how early we learn pride and self-reliance? That is exactly what got my boys to a place it turns out they didn't want to be, and it's what does the same thing to us.

Our pride makes us tell God, "No, I can do this myself. I have it figured out, and I don't need any help with this." And it's our pride that causes God to say in return, "OK, go for it. But when you get to where you want to be, don't forget to look down and see what you've gotten yourself into."

The Bible has a lot to say about how much God hates pride. James tells us how God responds to our pride: "But He gives a greater grace. Therefore it says, 'God is opposed to the proud, but gives grace to the humble'" (James 4:6).

In its original language, the word *opposed* in this verse is a military term that actually means God *goes after* the proud as an army would pursue its enemy. This tells us that God hates pride in His people so much that He aggressively and purposefully stands against the proud.

The Bible is very clear that God detests our pride and self-reliance. The Word is also very clear that God gives grace to those who will humble themselves in reliance on Him. If there is pride in your life, ask God to replace it with reliance on Him.

HERE'S WHAT I WANT YOU TO REMEMBER TODAY:

Pride is our enemy because it's God's enemy. We need to make sure our hearts are free of pride.

LAYING IT ALL AT HIS FEET

My younger son, Bryndan, is a tremendous baseball player. He loved playing the game, and he seems like a natural at it, too. He is so good, in fact, that he had numerous options after he graduated from high school. He was recruited to play ball for many colleges, and several of them offered him athletic scholarships.

I believe Bryndan could have had a fine college baseball career. However, God had other plans for my son.

During the latter part of Bryndan's junior year and all his senior year in high school, my wife, Karen, and I noticed that he had developed a real passion for evangelism. It seemed there was nothing he loved more than telling people about Jesus' love. God used Bryndan to share his faith with a number of his friends in school, and many of them trusted Christ as their Lord and Savior.

I was pleased but not surprised when Bryndan approached me during the second semester of his senior year to talk about his future. "Dad," he said, "I realize I need to make a decision about my future. I could play baseball in college, but I believe that God has called me to lay baseball on the altar."

That was quite a statement for a kid like Bryndan, a boy who had played baseball—and played it exceptionally well— since he turned out for the T-ball team when he was six years old. If it became clear to Bryndan that God wanted him to give up baseball, that's exactly what he intended to do.

As we prayed and talked about Bryndan's decision, we came to the conclusion that indeed God seemed to be confirming this new direction in his life. He turned down the offers to play college baseball and enrolled at Moody Bible Institute in Chicago, where he's preparing for full-time Christian work.

God calls each of us to do just as Bryndan did: place everything before Him as a sacrifice and an act of worship. God wants us to realize that nothing in this life belongs to us—including our plans for the future, our gifts, our talents, our hopes, and our dreams. These things are all on loan from God, and we've got to let Him do with them as He sees fit.

Jesus articulated this perspective with these words from the gospel of John:

> *Truly, truly, I say to you, unless a grain of wheat falls into the earth and dies, it remains alone; but if it dies, it bears much fruit. He who loves his life loses it, and he who hates his life in this world will keep it to life eternal. If anyone serves Me, he must follow Me; and where I am, there My servant will be also; if anyone serves Me, the Father will honor him.* (John 12:24–26)

Jesus is saying here that we must never come to Him asking Him to endorse what we want to do. Rather, we must come to Him laying everything—our talents, our skills, our desires, our plans and dreams—at the foot of the Cross so that He can use them as He will.

HERE'S WHAT I WANT YOU TO REMEMBER TODAY:

We need to pay attention when God calls us to do something. We shouldn't fight His call to lay aside our interests and ambitions for the sake of Christ and His Kingdom.

THE HOLY SPIRIT'S ROLE

I recently heard the story of a professing Christian man who divorced his wife to marry another woman, then justified his actions by saying that God told him to do it. When he was reminded about what the Scriptures say about the marriage covenant, he shrugged his shoulders and said, "What can I say? The Spirit of God told me to do this."

I don't doubt that a spirit told him to do what he did, but it wasn't the Holy Spirit. I can say that with certainty because I know that the Spirit will never tell us to do anything that violates or contradicts the written Word of God.

This might seem obvious for those of us who have read and understood the Scriptures, but there is, sadly enough, a tendency on all our parts to make subjective the objective statements of the Word of God. In other words, we will twist or ignore absolute truths in order to justify our wrong attitudes and actions.

The Holy Spirit speaks to us, prompts us, and urges us to do things He wants us to do. The way we know it is the Spirit speaking to us is that those promptings and urgings fall within the clear context and parameters of the Word of God. The Spirit will always direct us in ways that support the truths and directives of the Scriptures. It is His primary assignment to illuminate the Word to us and empower us to walk in obedience to the truths in the Word.

Here is what Jesus had to say about the role of the third member of the Trinity:

But when He, the Spirit of truth, comes, He will guide you into all the truth; for He will not speak on His own initiative, but whatever He hears, He will speak; and He will disclose to you what is to come. He will glorify Me, for He will take of Mine and will disclose it to you. All things that the Father has are Mine; therefore I said that He takes of Mine and will disclose it to you. (John 16:13–15)

Jesus assured us in this text that the Spirit of God supports and empowers the truth of the Word. Therefore, if we want direction, we need not and should not rely on our feelings or impulses. Instead we should go to the Word of God to see if we are going in the right direction.

Remember, the Spirit will *never* direct us to sin. He'll never have us leave our wives, commit adultery, lie, cheat, steal, or do any of the other things the Word tells us are wrong for the child of God.

The Enemy wants us to go through our earthly lives relying on our own desires and impulses. He wants us to either ignore what the written Word of God says or twist its truth to fit what we want.

Do you want to know if what you want is what God wants? Pray and ask the Spirit of God to illuminate the Scriptures for you. Then go to the Word and see what God has to say.

HERE'S WHAT I WANT YOU TO REMEMBER TODAY:

The Spirit of God will empower you to do what is right and in line with the truth of the Word of God.

STAYING FOCUSED

I've always loved baseball. I love keeping track of the scores and standings, and I love taking in a game when I can. I'd play the game now if I could. However, the normal wear and tear of age keeps me from getting out on the field. Although my body no longer allows me to play the game, I played when I was a teenager.

I remember one game in particular, and not fondly. The coach sent me out to play first base, a position I didn't usually play. On one play, a batter hit a grounder to our third-baseman, who scooped it up and threw it my way. It was a routine play—or so I thought.

The third-baseman made an accurate throw, and we would have had the runner easily. But for just a split second, I took my eye off the ball, and the ball glanced off the tip of my glove and hit me squarely in the mouth.

At the time, this incident demonstrated to me the importance of keeping my eye on the ball. Now it's an illustration that bad things can happen when you take your eye off what you are to be doing.

God has prepared each of us to follow a calling. He has given us spiritual gifts and talents, placed us in a location, put us in contact with certain people. Where we make our mistake is in looking away from where God has us and what He has us doing—taking our eye off the ball, as it were—and looking at what others are doing.

I would call that the "greener pastures" syndrome, and I believe it is a sin. I believe God wants each of us to be focused on Him and where He has us. When we take our eyes off Him, we risk losing out on the blessings He has for us.

Maybe the most recognizable example of this is the biblical account of Peter walking on the water. Peter started his walk just fine, as he kept his eyes on Jesus. But when he was distracted by the wind and waves, he sank.

A more tragic account of someone taking his eyes off his calling is found in the twenty-sixth chapter of 2 Chronicles. In this passage, we read of God using King Uzziah to usher in renewal and revival. God's blessing was on Uzziah, but he began looking at the calling of another:

> *But when he became strong, his heart was so proud that he acted corruptly, and he was unfaithful to the Lord his God, for he entered the temple of the Lord to burn incense on the altar of incense.*
> (2 Chronicles 26:16)

The problem here is that God had called Uzziah to be a king and not a priest. When he focused on the calling God had placed on him, blessings flowed to the people. But when he took his eyes off his calling, he suffered something far worse than a split lip or a wet robe—God punished him with leprosy.

We need to identify what God has called us to do and where He has called us to do it. Then we need to keep our focus on where He has us, and not look at others' places in this life.

HERE'S WHAT I WANT YOU TO REMEMBER TODAY:

Keep your eyes on your own calling, and you will receive God's blessing and empowerment.

RECEIVING FAVOR FROM GOD

My staff really has me pegged. They like to laugh at me and say, "Just give Crawford an excuse to celebrate, then get ready for the party."

OK, so they have me on that one. I really get a kick out of honoring people, out of making them feel good by recognizing something they've done well or something they add to the team at the office. I love sending staff members thank-you notes and cards to recognize something they have done. I like taking the whole staff out to lunch just to celebrate the blessing they are to me.

Before you get ready to nominate me for sainthood, I have to admit that I receive far more from those experiences than I could ever give. First of all, there's just something about my personality that loves a good party. I love the way I feel when we're in the midst of a good celebration, no matter how simple and small it may be. I like how it feels when those around me feel good about themselves and the job they are doing.

But it has occurred to me over the years that there is another benefit to honoring my staff, and it's what it does to their attitudes toward their work. Think about that for a minute. When your boss or some other authority honors you, what is usually your response? If you are like my staff, then you want to continue doing your best for that person. You want to do your best because you don't want to let down the one who has shown you that he believes in you and appreciates you.

I think the same principle applies in our relationship with God. When we do what's on God's heart, He moves closer to us. In effect, He honors us. And when the Lord honors us, we can't help but feel all the more motivated to please Him.

King David knew something about touching the heart of God by living a godly life: "But know that the Lord has set apart the godly man for Himself; the Lord hears when I call to Him" (Psalm 4:3).

The Lord "sets apart"—distinguishes from the rest of the pack—the godly man or woman who walks in integrity and consistently moves toward the heart of God. This doesn't mean these people are perfect (indeed, we know that David was not a man without his imperfections, yet God called the king "a man after God's own heart"), but they keep moving toward God, keep confessing and repenting, and keep walking toward His light.

I believe God sets that person aside and says of him or her, "This is a special one I want to honor. There's something about this person that represents Me."

David says, "The Lord hears when I call to Him." This expression means not only that God hears the godly person—the one who moves toward His heart—but that He gives that person His full attention.

Do you want God to honor you? Do you want to please God in your life? Then live a godly life by drawing closer and closer to Him.

HERE'S WHAT I WANT YOU TO REMEMBER TODAY:

We receive God's favor not by being perfect, but by drawing closer to His heart.

GIVING GOD THE LEFTOVERS?

My wife, Karen, has a gift and a talent for hospitality. There is nothing she likes better than to make our guests feel at home. She loves having people over, and she enjoys making guests feel special, as if they're the most important people in her life at that moment. She has a great sense of humor and a knack for conversation that puts our guests at ease.

Karen is great at getting the house and the meal ready before company arrives. She gets our home spotlessly clean, and she loves serving up a delicious, specially prepared meal. My wife would never consider serving leftovers to our guests. Karen loves to honor our guests, and to her serving leftovers is no way to do that. She wants to serve them the very best she has.

I think we have a tendency to give God our leftovers—our leftover time, our leftover energy, our leftover talents, our leftover money. We spend time in prayer and in His Word if we have time left at the end of the day. We worship God without distraction of our hearts and minds if we have the energy left. We give to His work if we have money left over after paying our bills and buying the things we want.

Obviously, these are examples of misplaced priorities. God spoke directly to this issue through the Old Testament prophet Malachi:

> "A son honors his father, and a servant his master. Then if I am a father, where is My honor? And if I am a master, where is My respect?' says the Lord of hosts to you, O priests who despise My name. But you say, 'How have we despised Your name?' You are pre-

senting defiled food upon My altar. But you say, 'How have we defiled You?' In that you say, 'The table of the Lord is to be despised.' But when you present the blind for sacrifice, is it not evil? And when you present the lame and sick, is it not evil? Why not offer it to your governor? Would he be pleased with you? Or would he receive you kindly?" says the Lord of hosts. (Malachi 1:6–8)

God is telling us in this passage that our best should go to Him first—not to our friends, not to our family, not to those we consider important. All that we have, all that we are, and all that we will ever be belongs to Him anyway, and giving it to Him puts it in its rightful place, where He can use it for His glory and our benefit.

The apostle Paul put it this way: "Therefore I urge you, brethren, by the mercies of God, to present your bodies a living and holy sacrifice, acceptable to God, which is your spiritual service of worship" (Romans 12:1).

When we offer God our bodies as living sacrifices, we give Him our very best right off the top, and that includes our time, our talents, our energy, our resources, our all.

HERE'S WHAT I WANT YOU TO REMEMBER TODAY:

Give to God first, and give Him your very best.

MAKING SOUND INVESTMENTS

I have a friend who pastors a very large church. I greatly respect his insights and wisdom, so one day I asked him, "What burdens you most about the American church?"

His answer came quickly, with the kind of conviction and intensity that told me he'd been thinking long and hard about the question I asked. "Consumerism and materialism," he said. "It is embarrassing, the amount of money we spend on ourselves to support lifestyles where more is never enough."

I couldn't agree with my friend more. Sadly, we live in an age of "rich religion," when those in the Christian community are as taken in by materialism as the rest of the world. It seems as if we have made a priority out of acquiring money and possessions, while at the same time there is such tremendous need out there. We live in a time when those in the church enjoy unprecedented material wealth. But at the same time countless ministries—and I'm talking about legitimate, effective ministries—struggle financially.

I don't believe this is just a blind spot on our parts; I believe it is a grievous sin in the church as a whole.

Now before you go out and sell everything you own and take a vow of poverty, hear me out. I don't believe money in and of itself is evil. I don't believe that working hard to make money is in and of itself wrong or sinful. I believe God wants us to enjoy life and provide for our families.

I'm talking about priorities here. I am talking about what we invest in and where we lay up our treasures. I believe God wants us to live comfortably and prepare for the future, but I

also believe we need to make investment—yes, including *financial* investment—in His kingdom our priority.

Jesus had plenty to say on this subject:

> *And He told them a parable, saying, "The land of a rich man was very productive. And he began reasoning to himself, saying, 'What shall I do, since I have no place to store my crops?' Then he said, 'This is what I will do: I will tear down my barns and build larger ones, and there I will store all my grain and my goods. And I will say to my soul, "Soul, you have many goods laid up for many years to come; take your ease, eat, drink and be merry."' But God said to him, 'You fool! This very night your soul is required of you;* and now who will own what you have prepared?' *So is the man who stores up treasure for himself, and is not rich toward God."* (Luke 12:16–21, emphasis added)

The principle here is that we are to give to that which lasts eternally, not just store up earthly treasures.

Each of us who has made Jesus Christ our Lord and Savior should ask God first to reveal to us the importance of investing in His kingdom. Then we should ask Him *how* He wants us to make those investments. Investments in the kingdom of God are the soundest investments we can make!

HERE'S WHAT I WANT YOU TO REMEMBER TODAY:

There's nothing wrong with planning for the future, but our priority should be to plan for and invest in eternity.

YOUR CALLING, YOUR PASSION

I'm indebted to a man by the name of Bobb Biehl, a consultant who travels around and helps Christian organizations and leaders to identify the vision God has placed on their hearts.

I heard Bobb speak several years ago, and he asked a question of those in attendance that God has anchored in my soul. "Gentleman," he asked, "what makes you pound the table and weep?"

In other words, what has God given you a passion, a vision, or a compelling sense of mission for? What really captures your heart?

From that day forward, I began to search my heart and evaluate my life and identify the burdens and passions I believed God had placed on my heart. I took the time to write those things down in my journal. To this day, when I feel in the least bit uncertain, I go back to that list and allow God to re-energize me to do what He has called me to do.

God has something special for each and every Christian to do. That is what we mean by the term "calling." There is no more satisfied, contented person than the one whose life is yielded to God's calling. And I believe that will can be found in the thing or things God gives us a burden and a passion for.

I think we Christians make finding our calling more complicated than it really needs to be. We seem to think that we'll receive our calling when the sky opens up, a light flashes down on us, and we hear a booming voice calling us into missionary work or some other ministry. Or we think we'll have some dream in which God shows us what we are to do with the rest of our lives.

Well, I believe God can communicate our calling any way

He wants to, but I also believe that the overwhelming majority of the time, He does it by placing within our hearts overwhelming burdens and passion—a sense of mission—for the calling He has for us. We can live lives of meaning and purpose when we pay attention to what He has placed on our hearts.

Late in the book of Acts, the apostle Paul explained what the calling of God looks like:

> *So, King Agrippa, I did not prove disobedient to the heavenly vision, but kept declaring both to those of Damascus first, and also at Jerusalem and then throughout all the region of Judea, and even to the Gentiles, that they should repent and turn to God, performing deeds appropriate to repentance.* (Acts 26:19–20)

Paul was talking about how he stayed on track when it came to what God had placed on his heart to do. He stayed true to the vision of declaring the Good News of Jesus Christ to the world around him. Paul was obedient to his calling, and God used the apostle in a mighty, world-changing way.

Do you want to know what God has called you to do? Do you want to know how you can change the world—or at least your part of the world—for Him? Then ask yourself where your passion is for Him. Ask yourself what makes you pound the table and weep.

HERE'S WHAT I WANT YOU TO REMEMBER TODAY:

Finding God's calling isn't as complicated as you might think. It's just a matter of the passion God has placed in your heart.
